EDUCATION TODAY

Musical Instruments
in the Classroom

EDUCATION TODAY

EDUCATION TODAY: LANGUAGE TEACHING

For a full list of titles in this series, see back cover

Musical Instruments in the Classroom

GEOFFREY WINTERS GRSM LRAM

Senior Lecturer in Music
Balls Park College of Education

LONGMAN

LONGMAN GROUP LIMITED
London

Associated companies, branches and representatives
throughout the world

© *Geoffrey Winters* 1967

First published 1967
Third impression 1972

ISBN 0 582 32062 3

Printed in Malta by
St Paul's Press Ltd

Contents

Acknowledgements

We are grateful to the following for permission to reproduce copyright material:

J. Curwen & Sons Ltd for *Masters in this Hall*, words by W. Morris (French tune); Dr Maud Karpeles for the tune *Nancy's Fancy* from *Country Dance Tunes*, Set 2, collected by Cecil J. Sharp (Novello, London), and Oxford University Press for *Ach, du lieber Augustin* and *Ball Gawn Roun'* from *Oxford School Music Book 2*.

I

By Way of Introduction

Let me start by establishing two fundamental points. First, that what is outlined in this book in no way is a substitute for the class singing lesson, but is frequently a partner to it, and second, that nearly all the instrumental work suggested can be carried out with instrumental skills largely practised during the lesson and therefore excludes no child who is willing to 'have a go'.

We are not sure whether early man 'sang' or 'banged' first, but we *are* sure that both singing and playing are basic needs in our full development, and this book's aim is to widen instrumental activity in the classroom. It assumes only a little musical knowledge on the part of the teacher and, as will be shown, a class capable of performing its own song accompaniments will be a great help to the less capable teacher-pianist who so often struggles with the instrument when attention to the singing is needed far more. Apart even from this consideration, so many songs are all the better for a light accompaniment on instruments other than the piano—for instance a couple of notes on chime bars, the addition of a plucked open string on the 'cello, an easy chord from the guitar, a gay interpolation by the tambourine, not to mention a bang on the drum at an appropriate place, or a descant or second part on a few (please note few) recorders. Whilst speaking of accompaniments, it must be emphasized that they must never swamp the voices, or even make it necessary for voices to be forced, and although this is a book on instrumental work I would add that some songs (just occasionally) are better unaccompanied.

It will be found in practice that the various instrumental methods are adaptable for all ages from five to fifteen and will readily appeal even in the secondary stage if a little slant is given towards the guitar or the drums, especially combined with a degree of 'off-beat' rhythm. By these means boys in particular, who might otherwise take little interest in the subject, are encouraged to take an active part. A wide range is catered for, not only in age but also in ability. Members of a less able class will really come to life if they are asked to provide an improvised background to a song or to test each other with patterns played on a drum. A brighter class may eventually write and perform a fairly complex composition. It is important in respect of age and ability to move from strength to strength with success gained through careful attention to well graded assignments. No real progress is made when everything is such a struggle that most of the children despair and cease to enjoy themselves. Start with straightforward ideas which can immediately be taken up and performed with enthusiasm, and develop from there.

One of the important results of instrumental work, as with singing, is the joy of doing something together. As the improvisations, accompaniments or ensembles develop there is the special feeling of contributing a vital part, even if it is only an occasional first beat on a triangle or mysterious rasp on the scraper. The children must be encouraged to listen to the effect of adding another instrumental timbre and help to decide how much of a particular colour is desirable—this will add importance even to the most humble of contributors. Besides the use of simple instruments that can be readily mastered during the lesson, an important contribution is often provided and a useful outlet found for the talents and acquired skills of those who have studied instruments extramurally. Members of the recorder class are most helpful; string players, the occasional pianist or brass player come in at the secondary level; all can play a valuable part—although, as was stated at the beginning, the object is to be able to do something worthwhile without this 'stiffening' from outside sources. The resulting mixed ensembles are often much more interesting and readily appealing than the single colour groups—strings, recorders, brass etc. They are without a doubt far more adventurous and stimulating than percussion bands, where instruments are multiplied indiscriminately and even then are not self-sufficient, depending as they do on the gramophone or piano to provide the tune and harmony.

Further, these simple beginnings in class are often the vital spark that stimulates a child to venture further with music. A pupil given a violin to pluck an open string ostinato might discover a genuine affinity with the instrument and ask to pursue it further. The incidental tinklings of a youngster on the glockenspiel may well lead to a desire to learn some other instrument, or perhaps to start to write music. In these days of ready-made, canned music, in which the television in the living-room has supplanted the piano (long since, perhaps, used for firewood) a boy or girl often is quite old before he or she can manage to enjoy himself 'playing about' on an instrument. This is certainly one example of deprivation in an affluent society.

Many children may be heard to improvise vocally to themselves, in the bath or lying in bed, for example, but it is usually difficult to persuade them to use their voices in this way in front of other children. But give them an instrument and perhaps set a group rhythmic background going and they will express themselves more readily. Those who have fewer ideas are often helped with a suggestion as to rhythm, or their imagination is fired if they are asked to provide appropriate musical illustrations to a story. This method is ideal for using several children, especially if a story is selected with a large number of characters and recurring incidents.

From these efforts at improvisation, and from the class work on accompaniments and ensemble pieces, children are easily led on to writing and arranging their own pieces. This is a most valuable facet of their musical training and power of expression, and one which has been largely neglected until recently. Some advice in this connection is given towards the end of the book; it is largely a matter of subtly guiding the pupil, so that what he attempts can be fully realised with the resources available.

At this point it must be said that the instrumental field of music-making is the ideal foundation from which to encourage children in the skill of music-reading. So often this cart is put before the horse. Nobody asks a baby to read before it can talk, but frequently the school child is asked to learn about the complex sphere of notation before he can see any necessity for doing so and before he has the musical vocabulary to make the work have meaning. It can be a difficult task to make a child realise the desirability of being able to sight-sing, and, unless some convincing reason can be shown, progress is likely to be slow—after all, we hope he has

3

learnt his songs by rote from the cradle, and the change to learning them himself often seems without point. It is true that he can and should learn much of the early instrumental work by simple imitation, but as the pieces lengthen or become more complex, or require a greater degree of cooperation with others, the need and reason for notational prompts grows—this is the incentive to start music-reading. This order has a sound historical basis.

The cost of equipping a music department with an array of instruments can be considerable, especially if all that is inherited from a previous era are a few jingleless tambourines, snareless drums and beaterless triangles. Guidance on basic requirements is given in the following chapter and in Appendix C, but here it may be mentioned that much is possible in the way of home-made instruments of a simple nature which need only elementary skill, and that with more careful craftsmanship more advanced instruments can be made, such as xylophones and pipes.

The methods described in the following chapters have all grown from classroom practice in both primary and secondary schools. Some on paper may seem rather impracticable at first reading, but they have all worked. Discipline will generally grow naturally from the activity itself, but for a few lessons paddle in the shallow end with an odd xylophone, or tambourine and rattle; do not dive off the top board with an instrument for everyone. This will give the class and the teacher a chance to evolve the best method of organisation as the work proceeds. Sometimes the various groups will need time to practise; often it is desirable to allow time for experimental activity. These are both cases of time well spent, but they are noisy. Let a quiet word drop in the staff room—or mention it to the colleague in the next room and perhaps advise the Head of the general idea—otherwise some embarrassment may arise until all are used to this apparently strange but far from unrewarding music-making.

No book on instrumental work in the classroom could be written without in some way being indebted to Carl Orff. The present author owes much to the pioneer work of Orff, but hopes that the original material arising from his own experience will be discernible also. Those familiar with the teachings of Orff will realise that the approach and balance in the present volume are different, and perhaps more readily applicable to music in this country, where our native folk music has been less dominated by tonic-dominant than has that of Germany. Therefore the need to dwell quite so lengthily in the pentatonic sphere as an antidote, as in the Orff school music books, is less pressing.

The chapters form a logical sequence for the development of instrumental skills, but naturally the material overlaps and it is not necessary to work through the whole of a chapter before proceeding to the next. For instance, after a simple improvisation has been stimulated, the same might be added to a song or, after practice at a three note ostinato has been given, it might be combined with an improvisation. If one is a complete novice at this type of music-making it is a good plan to get together with two or three children in the dinner hour and try a few ideas out.

All that is mentioned in the following pages will widen the horizons of the music lesson—the aim is to allow every child to experience the joy of making music as opposed to listening passively. Couple this with a healthy approach to singing, and the class will achieve vital appreciation and delight in music.

2

The Instruments

Instruments for use in the classroom cover a wide range in timbre and type and are capable also of being played with satisfaction by children with widely varying natural ability. Some require greater skill than others, but there surely will not be a single child in any class who is incapable of making some instrumental contribution to the music lesson. Some instruments, for instance the percussion section and the so-called 'Orff' instruments, will be used to their full potential; others such as the recorders may be limited to a simple scale or even three notes, string instruments to open strings only and a guitar to a single chord, but all will add their particular colour and help the pupil to savour some of the essence of active music-making.

For convenience we will divide the available instruments into three flexible groups as follows: those instruments most suited to playing a melody, those which most easily provide chords or a bass part and lastly the multifarious instruments that contribute a rhythmic background.

Melodic instruments

Into the first group come the tuned percussion instruments (such as the glockenspiels and xylophones), the recorders, the harmonicas and melodicas. Naturally any other instrument capable of melody also comes into this category, but only those that can be learnt with comparative ease will be discussed in this section. Mention will be made of the strings, guitar and the piano in the next group where they may be used in a limited manner to provide a bass or a few chords. Chime bars are also better deferred, although they can be arranged in the form of a glockenspiel for melodic work.

MELODIC PERCUSSION

In introducing the tuned percussion family some generalisation will be necessary, as there is a wide choice of instruments available, varying considerably in nomenclature and range. It is best, if funds will permit, to buy the best, as quality in instruments is generally rewarding. This is not to say that many of the more competitively priced instruments are not perfectly serviceable (although their tone quality is often inferior), but they should be checked carefully for intonation—especially the xylophones. Reference to the British Standards Institution's books and kite marks is a safeguard.

All the instruments consist of bars (with their names engraved) either of metal or wood mounted on a frame. Some are without resonators, whilst others have a box resonator; the more expensive and larger chromatic models have individual tube resonators. All are played with pairs of sticks which have either wooden, rubber or felt heads.

GLOCKENSPIELS AND METALLOPHONES

The highest, sounding two octaves higher than written, are the small or soprano glockenspiels, sometimes also referred to as dulcimers. (The term dulcimer should strictly apply to the stringed zither-type instrument and in this book is reserved for that instrument.) They are played with wooden or rubber beaters and have ranges of an octave to an octave and a half, starting an octave or two octaves above middle C.

Next in pitch are the large or alto glockenspiels. They start an octave above middle C and have a range of $1\frac{1}{2}$ or 2 octaves (sounding an octave higher than written). Some makes include the B below the C in their range.

Surprisingly, the cheaper models have box resonators, but the more expensive are only frame mounted. This is because the more expensive instruments with box resonators are known as metallophones and have ranges starting an octave lower than middle C. They are played with felt-headed beaters.

All the glockenspiels are available in a diatone or chromatic

7

form. The former have the equivalent of the white keys of the piano and the only complete major scale available is in the key of C. The chromatic models have the semitones formed by the black keys on the piano and are thus playable in any key. If the piece does not require black notes it can be played on a diatonic model, and in addition some diatonic models include additional F sharps and B flats that may be substituted when playing in keys other than C. The substitution is possible by means of removable bars which also permit the number of notes presented to the child to be limited, at the discretion of the teacher, to those actually required for any one piece or improvisation.

The metallophone is, in its simplest form (i.e. with a box resonator) a diatonic instrument, with the extra F sharp and B flat. If a chromatic model is required it is available with the individual tube resonators and is accordingly considerably more expensive.

XYLOPHONES

The wooden instruments are known only as xylophones. The bars should be made of rosewood, if they are to have a really satisfactory tone. Most manufacturers market a diatonic model with changing notes F sharp and B flat, but a chromatic model, with individual resonators is also available. The soprano model starts an octave above middle C and has a range of about an octave and a half; the tenor-alto has about a two-octave range, starting from middle C, and the bass has F in the bass stave as its lowest note. Xylophones generally sound best if played with felt beaters, but brilliant sounds may be obtained with wooden or rubber beaters. (Naturally the bass and tenor instruments will be used principally for the lower parts rather than melodic work; they have been mentioned her for the sake of completeness.)

The choice of instrument—metal or wood—will be dictated by the quality of sound needed for any particular situation, and the following general points on tone quality will be a guide to their usage. On many occasions they are interchangeable and a matter of individual preference. Large glockenspiels and metallophones are resonant, bell-like and full in tone, and are best used for slower moving passages. The small glockenspiels are considerably less resonant and therefore drier in effect, making their most effective contribution in quicker moving melodies. Xylophones are either mysterious, if played gently, or striking and penetrating in sound if played more crisply. Their sound fades more quickly than the metal instruments, but they add a precise rhythmic emphasis and are useful for quick tunes.

The instruments are played as mentioned earlier with a pair of beaters, which should not be held too firmly, but allowed to rebound lightly from the keys after striking. If they are left in contact, the sound is stopped or damped. This is necessary when rests occur, or at the end of a piece, or when the sound continuing clouds the harmony. Under these circumstances the sounds are damped by stopping the vibration of the key with the fingers or hand. Professionals use the beaters very largely alternately, but the layout of the passage will generally dictate the most suitable and comfortable hand to use. Certainly single hand playing should be discouraged from the beginning, as it will be found that well conceived tuned percussion music lends itself to alternate beater technique.

Other Melodic Instruments

RECORDERS

The recorder family consists of six instruments, pitched either in the key of C or F, which range in size from the tiny sopranino to the great bass. For our purposes most use will be made of the common but versatile descant recorder and some reference will be made to the tenor. Both descant and tenor are 'C' instruments, which means that their lowest note and basic scale is C—the descant sounding an octave higher than written. The tenor is selected as an alternative for our purposes, in preference to the treble, despite the need for larger hands, because it is possible to transfer straight from the descant to the tenor without having to learn new fingering.

Many children will learn the recorder in a separate class but even those who do not are usually able to acquire quickly the ability to play the first and easiest five notes. All these are played with the left-hand fingers only and are usually best taught in the order B, A, G then C and D.

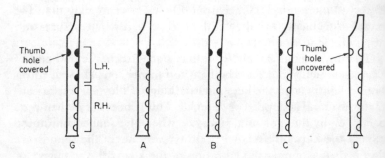

It is important to impress the necessity for a soft, gentle attack, secured by commencing each note with a 't'. (This is known as tonguing.) If the pupil is already acquainted with French time-names it is possible to transfer these directly to the tonguing technique.

When proficiency has been gained on five notes, a wide range of melodic work becomes possible before it is necessary or desirable to proceed to the more difficult lower notes produced with the help of the right-hand fingers.

Descant recorders are not expensive to buy and many good plastic models are catalogued by instrument manufacturers. A plastic recorder, apart from its tendency to break if dropped, usually proves a more satisfactory instrument than a cheap wooden model. However a 'concert' wooden model is available for under £2. Reference to B.S.I. leaflets is recommended. Naturally, as with all wind instruments, it is better that a child should have his own, but if this is not possible the question of using the school's can be overcome with a jarful of some mild disinfectant such as T.C.P. for dipping the mouthpiece.

MOUTH ORGANS OR HARMONICAS

Into our melodic group come also the harmonicas and their close but more expensive relatives the melodicas. These instruments blend well with the other instruments, but the harmonicas need to be individually owned as they cannot be easily cleaned; the thought of blowing into an instrument used by someone else is unpleasant but the thought of drawing the air through such an instrument is even more so. Harmonicas are made in two- or three-octave models, chromatic (with a slide) or diatonic. The usual school instruments are pitched in C (although they conveniently include down to bottom soh in their range) and are played by blowing in for notes of the doh chord (i.e. C, E, G and C) or drawing in the air for the other notes, D, F, A and B.[1] Hence a scale of C is produced as follows: (hole 1) 'blow-suck', (hole 2) 'blow-suck', (hole 3) 'blow-suck', and (hole 4) 'suck-blow'. Incidentally holes 4 and 5 both give the note C when blown but give B and D respectively when drawn.

| G | C | C | E | G | C | C | E | G | C | Blow |
| A | B | D | F | A | B | D | F | A | B | Suck |

The holes are isolated by one of three methods: first and easiest, by 'blocking out' (covering up) with the fingers those holes not required; second, by 'pointing the mouth' as in whistling, and third, usually requiring a great deal of practice, by blocking the holes not required with the tongue. The chromatic slide has a similar effect to that of a valve on a brass instrument; when it is pressed in, it raises the whole compass a semitone.

MELODICAS

The Melodicas are very much mongrels. The tone is produced by metal reeds as in the harmonica; they are held somewhat like a recorder and they have a keyboard arrangement like a piano, which allows chords to be played. They are expensive, the cheapest being over £5, but have the advantage over the harmonicas that they produce immediate results 'with the press of a finger and a gentle blow', as opposed to the blow or drawing and blocking of unwanted holes. They blend well and are a useful additional tone colour. Their range is two octaves and either starts on middle C (or B) or, in the case of the alto, F below middle C.

[1] Vaughan Williams uses these two chords to evoke the sound of a mouth organ in the 'London Symphony', 3rd movement.

Chord Instruments

CHIME BARS

We come now to perhaps the most versatile of the class instruments, the chime bars. These, like the French horn in the symphony orchestra, which is often associated with the woodwind but is equally happy with the brass, are as much at home playing the melody or the harmony. Because they are readily portable, a single note can be handed to a child who can either play part of a melody or, perhaps more suitably, a note of a chord at the appropriate place. Used in this way, with just two chords (tonic and dominant seventh, that is doh and soh) seven children can be actively and joyfully employed in contributing a valuable harmonic basis.

Various makes of chime bars are available and range in price, largely according to size, from 60p to £1.25 each. The lowest bar is the G below middle C and the highest two and a half octaves above middle C. Basically they consist of a metal bar mounted over a resonator which is either rectangular or round. They are played and sound like the glockenspiel.

Many instruments mentioned in this chapter are optional; chime bars are almost indispensable.

PIANO

The piano, it must be admitted straight away, blends less well with the other instruments, in particular the pitched percussion, but against this must be set the fact that it is found in most schools, that it provides basic chords fairly easily, and that it is a great favourite with the children, who in these days seldom have one at home and consider it a privilege to play on an instrument often reserved for the teacher. It needs no introduction, but care must be taken that the tuner tunes it to the correct pitch, otherwise it will certainly not blend with any of the tuned percussion or with the recorders. More will be said in a later chapter about the method of arranging for it, but here it is worth noting that the chord layout must be simple and that very often it is best to use two players, one concentrating on the chords or figuration normally played by the right hand, the other managing the bass (probably only two or three notes).

GUITAR

The majority of children are only too willing to play any of the fretted instruments and these particularly come into their own at the secondary level. Some juniors can manage a guitar, but it is usually better to use ukeleles for younger children, as the stretches for chords are so much less taxing. The guitar should be of the Spanish type, preferably with nylon strings, as although these are soft, they are pleasanter in quality and infinitely less cruel to the fingers, especially of the left hand. A worthwhile guitar should cost from about £15; it will be most useful and will win its way to the hearts of secondary boys, who will soon overcome their disappointment that it is quite a normal shape and has no wires to plug in. They may even come to prefer its more retiring ways to those of its more raucous cousin. In the chapter on basic chords some consideration will be given to the method of playing and to a small repertoire of chords. The instrument is tuned in fourths, except between the second and third strings where the interval is a third.

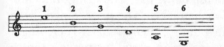

Incidentally, for convenience it is written an octave higher than it sounds, when staff notation is used, but for our purposes we shall use only chord diagrams. The highest *sounding* string is the first; confusion will almost certainly arise and must be patiently overcome, as unfortunately this highest sounding string is *lowest* when the instrument is in its usual playing position.

UKELELE

A valuable introduction to guitar technique is provided by the ukelele which has only four strings and is considerably smaller. The four strings are in fact tuned to an 'added sixth' chord (so beloved at one time by Tin Pan Alley) but their actual pitch is usually considered to be variable and in music that has a ukelele

part one sees an instruction at the beginning of the piece such as:
Tune ukelele to

The method of tuning where the fourth string is higher than the third or second is known as re-entrant tuning. The result of tuning in this way is that close harmony chords are easily played. Most commonly it is tuned A D F sharp B or a tone lower G C E A according to the key of the piece. It is always notated with chord diagrams. Its close relative, the banjo, has a much more 'twangy' and penetrating sound due to the drum-like body of the instrument.

AUTOHARP

At this point reference might be made to the 'autoharp'. A very mechanical instrument, closely related to the zither, having twenty to thirty strings which might absorb an interesting, but possibly exasperating half hour in being tuned. The strings are mostly played by being strummed, and pleasant but quiet chords are produced by depressing a bar which damps out strings foreign to the chord indicated on the top of the bar. The strings may also be played with small wooden hammers. The price ranges from £7 to £12 and determines the number of chord bars. There might be three only, or as many as twelve. A useful instrument that is easy to play.

DULCIMERS AND PSALTERIES

These instruments have a harp-like tone and are basically a number of strings, which are tunable, stretched over a resonating box. They are mentioned at this point, as a useful chordal dulcimer is on the market which has its strings grouped in threes to provide the most frequently occurring chords; they may be used equally for melodic work and provide a pleasing extra tone colour. The strings are played either with a felt hammer or by plucking with the fingers. Their range is usually about an octave and a half from just below middle C, and they are available in chromatic or diatonic form at prices from about £8. Simple dulcimers are

14

suitable for home construction and details will be found in the books mentioned in Appendix D.

STRINGS

Open strings played pizzicato, or occasionally with a bow, provide ideal bass notes for the other instruments in our ensembles. Some schools may be fortunate enough to possess a double bass. Failing this the 'cello is admirable, as it has a pleasant resonance which combines well with the other instruments. A viola makes a good substitute, and even the violin, especially the lower two strings, provides a satisfactory bass to instruments such as descant recorders and glockenspiels, whose ranges are high.

Digression on keys

It is worth noticing the notes that are available as open strings: A D G and low C on the 'cello and viola, E A D and the G below the treble stave on the violin. The double bass also tunes to the notes E A D and G but in its case the E is the lowest note. These notes, as will be explained later, are all root notes to the three most important chords, Tonic, Dominant, Sub-Dominant, or doh, soh and fah respectively, in the keys of G and D. Couple this with the fact that by far the easiest key in which to play the recorder is G, and also that this key is easy on the tuned percussion instruments, and it becomes clear that this is a suitable basic key for our particular activities. The key of D is only slightly more difficult, having two sharps. Now it also happens that these two keys are likely choices for songs, as they have comfortable vocal ranges: D to D in the key of D is doh to doh and the same notes in G fall between soh and lower soh; think for example of:

Hot cross buns   Baa, baa black sheep have you a - ny wool

The key of C indisputably has its advantages, being all white notes on keyboard instruments and requiring no key signature when we come to the writing stage, but against these one has to set the fact that it is a tricky key on a descant recorder, as the lowest note is not very effective as well as being difficult to produce, and the note F is an awkward note to finger. Also for most infants and juniors the key of C is too low for singing and there is a tendency to force the weak lower notes, which must be discouraged.

This short digression is by way of a justification for the large percentage of examples in this book quoted in the keys of G and D.

TIMPANI

To return to the instruments we come to the last, but far from least in size or popularity (or regrettably price) of our group of harmonic or bass instruments: the timpani or kettledrums. So useful and enjoyable will a pair of timpani be found that it is well worth putting on a special concert, or a jumble sale, or 'getting round the Head', or the Parents Association, or even making a direct approach to the county music adviser, in order to procure them. To come to hard 'brass' facts they are known as 'junior or school timpani' and range in price from approximately £15 to £21 per drum or with a more elaborate tuning system from £24 to £30. To this you will need to add just over £1.50 for a pair of sticks—I forgot on the first occasion I ordered for my school. Traditionally the drums are tuned (which will require practice) to doh and soh —whether the small or large one is tuned doh and the other accordingly top or bottom soh will depend on the particular model of drum and the key of the piece. The stretch of the skin varies with the humidity, so pray for settled weather, especially if a concert is planned. When tuning press firmly in the middle of the skin with the palm of the hand to even up the tension. You will soon learn how much to turn each screw-tap to bring the drum up or down the required amount in pitch. The tuning process is an excellent source of aural training for the teacher and the class, and the drums provide an ideal bass to all our instruments as well as being 'hot favourites' for free improvisation and imitation exercises. When playing the timpani the player should aim to use the two sticks in such a way that the heads strike an area no bigger than a sixpence on the skin—this ensures that the pitch of each stroke is identical and also that the skin vibrates equally. It will also be found that the timpani make an admirable medium for an introduction to note-reading—two notes only! Start planning

16

your approach to the economic issue now—you will never regret it.

(I note that tunable tambours at nearly £4 each are marketed by one school music shop—they may make a cheaper substitute.)

Other percussion

Finally we arrive at the purely rhythmic instruments which probably need less introduction. Briefly the group comprises the following well-known instruments: drums (side and bass), tambourines, cymbals, triangles and bells, jingles and castanets.

Less well known (or perhaps more true to say less commonly found outside the dance-hall) we have bongo-drums which are rather expensive, tom-toms, maracas, wood blocks, claves and the reso-reso or scraper. Go to a good school instrument supplier and have a happy morning trying a few out, but try to afford instruments, not 'toys'. For example, you can buy a triangle for 2s 6d but you may consider in the long run that a more expensive one, at say 10s., will give greater satisfaction to the user and listener.

Many of the instruments mentioned in this chapter are fairly easily made at school, especially those found in the last group. If you decide to try your hand, do it in the craft lesson, not in the small proportion of time usually allocated to music. (Do not show this sentence to the craft specialist.) Experiment—and for guidance refer to the books mentioned in Appendix D.

If the reader feels unable to make a choice from the wide range mentioned, I have listed in Appendix C suggestions for starting with various amounts of money. Once a basic collection has been formed, it is easy and not too expensive to expand.

3
From Imitation to Improvisation

The music lesson often provides too little opportunity for the child to express his own ideas in musical terms. Improvisation consists of making up rhythmic and melodic phrases out of one's own imagination on an instrument suitable for this purpose, or with one's voice or, in the case of rhythmic improvisation, perhaps only with hands or feet. It is a valuable starting point for our use of instruments, as it requires no previous knowledge of notation and its technical demands are always directly related to the ability of the improvisor.

Sixty years ago improvisation must have been a lost art. Now jazz musicians have shown the way and serious musicians have revived the art as practised in the seventeenth and eighteenth centuries and have, with indeterminacy in *avant-garde* music, made it an important element in the field of serious music. It is worth noting that as the composer became more concerned with the exact way his music was to be performed, so he left less and less to the performer's imagination and taste. In Bach's day the keyboard continuo was improvised on the framework of a ground bass provided by the composer, but by the time we arrive at Beethoven we find that although in the early works he left the cadenzas to be extemporized by the particular performer, in the later concerti he writes the cadenzas himself. Perhaps he had suffered the experience of having a composition ruined by a performer's badly conceived cadenza.

A valid criticism of improvisation is that it becomes formally out of hand and may wander indefinitely and aimlessly throughout its length.

This chapter is concerned primarily with ways of helping the child to command the means of expressing himself on an instrument in an extempore manner. It suggests ways of extending his ability and developing his sense of form; it also points the way to

18

collective improvisations. These aims do not exclude the occasion when it is a good thing to allow the pupil to experiment quite freely with an instrument purely for his own satisfaction and recreation.

Returning to jazz, it will probably be well known that individual players improvise melodically over a very definite harmonic framework. This use of a framework is the essence of developing the art of improvisation in the classroom. The framework may be in the form of a suggestion about time, phrase length (e.g. improvise a rhythmic accompaniment to the verse of a song), range of notes, basic harmony, or other limitations, but the work produced within such a framework will have a considerable diversity and vitality, because it is built on a satisfactory ground plan.

Rhythmic imitation

We can best lay the foundations of improvisation by extensive use of imitation, as by this means the children acquire a vocabulary of rhythmic patterns that they can then use in their own way. The first steps provide a stimulating activity in any lesson and seem to be equally enjoyed at any age.

1 Set a pulse rate by tapping quietly with the foot.
2 Clap a two-bar phrase to the class.

$\frac{2}{4}$ ♩ ♫ ♩ ♩ ‖

3 The class clap it back.
4 Straightaway clap the next phrase.

$\frac{2}{4}$ ♩ ♫ ♫♩ ‖

5 They clap it back and so we proceed.

These phrases may be as simple or as complicated (with syncopation and rests) as you want, but there must be no break in the continuity—neither class nor teacher must hesitate when it is their turn. When clapping notes that are longer than one beat, the effect of the note continuing can be simulated by holding the hands together and moving them once for each extra beat without clapping, e.g. a three-beat note would be: clap–hold–hold. Alternatively the concept of rests might be introduced and instead of trying to clap a three-beat note, one could clap once and follow with two one-beat rests which could be indicated either by nodding or with foot taps. As their imitative memory improves, increase the phrases in length, or use three or four beats in a bar. Variety can be added by slapping the knees or sides, or by stamping with the feet. This contributes greatly to the enjoyment whilst at the same time requiring increased control. It also develops an appreciation of different aural tone colours.

Again we must remember that this is all made up as we go along and the children in the class respond to this ever-evolving improvisation. The next stage is to ask for a volunteer to take over the role of the teacher and improvise phrases for the class to repeat. There will be no shortage of recruits and plenty of useful practice will result. It is usually appreciated if the teacher joins the class at this stage and this also helps to keep the beat going.

A variation of the game 'Mrs O'Grady Says' can be played with the above. It consists of instructing the class to listen for the same phrase clapped twice running, if this occurs, either they should not answer and possibly fold their arms, or perhaps they could clap some prearranged phrase, such as four equal beats. The former keeps everyone on their toes, as no one likes to be caught out clapping when he should be silent.

Rhythmic Question and Answer

From these early games of imitation an appreciation of rhythmic possibilities and phrase lengths will grow. We follow direct imitation, with the development of the technique of question and answer.

Clap a phrase to a child—

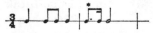

* The dotted rhythm is more difficult and should be used with discretion, but it does add considerable vitality when introduced.

Instead of imitating this, the child answers with a phrase of a similar nature that provides a logical and convincing answer, for example:

Either you should look at a child at random or go round the class in order. When they are quite used to this, each pupil can ask his neighbour or someone else on the opposite side of the class a question and expect a reasonable answer straight away. Keep the class ticking steadily—no stops between question and answer, nor between each pair. This may seem a lengthy procedure, but if a little calculation is done, it will be noted that, without stops a two-bar phrase and its answer in 2/4 at ♩ = 100 (a comfortable speed for this work), will take a class of forty children only one and three-fifths minutes.

Group work

Orff suggests the use of words as a stimulant to rhythmic invention and as a framework on which to build group improvisations. Any names may be taken, girls, boys, teachers, flowers, cars, instruments and so on. These are recited against a regular beat provided by clapping, slapping or stamping. Again it must be emphasized that it is most important that a regular pulse be established, as in all the ideas outlined in this chapter. The class may be divided into groups and the work performed antiphonally or contrapuntally. If we take the names of towns as our subject, the effect would be as follows:

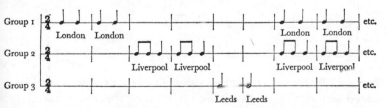

To the same rhythm some children might add percussion instruments. Perhaps a drum for London, a cymbal clashed for Leeds and a tambourine or maracas for Liverpool. By careful choice of subject, this activity can be enjoyed by any age group. For those who have a rudimentary knowledge of notation, a simple score may be prepared, and this makes a good introduction to the more elaborate scores that will be needed for instrumental ensembles.

Improvised percussion accompaniments

When a repertoire of rhythmic patterns has been assimilated we can use them as simple percussion accompaniments to songs that the children know. If the class has learnt a song such as *Bobby Shafto*, a child might be invited to choose an instrument, such as a woodblock or tambourine, and encouraged first to tap the beat only, to a verse and then perhaps to add a little extra where he feels it is suitable; for example, where the voice has a one-beat note, the accompanist might keep things going with a ta-te.

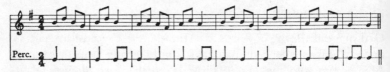

There will be time for quite a number of children to have a turn during the normal singing lesson, especially if they are limited to one or two verses each. Later two or perhaps three children could share a verse, each having a different instrument. As an example, look at the following treatment of *This Old Man*.

It must not be forgotten that although these examples are illustrated in notation, at this stage we are concerned with the child making up his own accompaniments as he goes along: nothing should be written. Some children might be helped by taking a word or phrase from a song and using its rhythm for the instrumental part. For example, in *This Old Man* the word 'paddywhack' would provide an exciting and entertaining off-beat rhythm.

More will be said later about the use of words as a stimulant to rhythm. These three examples will give sufficient idea of the possibilities of this simple but enjoyable and effective method of improvisation and we will now turn to the methods of imitation which will contribute so much to the basic training of the pupil.

Melodic imitation and Question and Answer

When a start has been made with rhythmic imitation and answering, the same methods may be employed with melodic work. Orff recommends starting on the notes G and E which form a natural interval that occurs in the pentatonic scale, which is discussed later in this chapter, when group melodic work is elaborated. This forms a sound basis for progress.

In the early stages limit the tunes to two sounds; timpani tuned to doh and soh provide an excellent medium for this, or alternatively open strings on a guitar or 'cello. Chime bars might be used either on adjacent notes or forming an interval. Proceed as follows:

1 Select the instruments and the notes to be played.
2 Play a short two-bar phrase.
3 Class sing it back.
4 On the same two notes play a second phrase.
5 Class sing it back.

When you have shown the way, let the children take it in turns to set the problem. Here are some of the ideas they might be expected to produce.

23

On a timpani tuned to doh and soh.

On a guitar using open strings 2 and 3.

On chimes using adjacent notes.

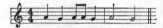

On chimes using stranger notes.

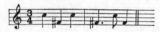

After this, if there are sufficient instruments, let a child imitate the phrase on an instrument instead of the class singing. The instruments need not be the same, provided they can play the same notes, or at least the same notes in a different octave.

When proficiency has been gained with two notes, move on to three. Any of the following make suitable note combinations, but of course others should be used as well. The possibilities are quite extensive, and no attempt should be made to move on to more notes until the children are able to improvise and imitate melodies with just three.

They will also enjoy asking each other questions with short melodic phrases. Again start with two notes only and then add a third. Here are two examples of a Question and Answer with two and then three notes.

After this add more notes, say the first five notes of the scale.

Up to this point the feeling for doh is unlikely to make itself felt, but when part of a scale is used, as with five notes, the last player will probably feel the need to end on doh. Then they will realize that the question sounds more like a question if it ends on a sound other than doh.

Notice the unity given by the same rhythm for question and answer—most children will instinctively realize that this is effective, but naturally the teacher must commend more highly those who manage to overcome the monotony of an exact rhythmic imitation with a subtle variation, as in the next example.

When the children have become good at this, we can build towards longer pieces. Let four children have glockenspiels or other available instruments and ask the first to play a tune, the second to answer it, the third to play as nearly as possible the first tune and the fourth to answer that. The result is a tune in A B A C form and a similar procedure could be used for A A B A form. If there are not enough instruments to do this, some of the phrases could be sung.

Group improvisation

Practice in improvisation is also possible at this stage antiphonally between the class and a soloist. Generally speaking the class will clap or slap their knees and the soloist will improvise on a rhythmic or melodic instrument. One way is for the class to clap a pre-arranged phrase and for the soloist to perform a balanced but contrasting phrase: alternatively, the soloist plays a melodic phrase and the class claps back the rhythm. A further development of these methods is for the class to divide, one group answering the soloist's rhythm exactly and the other group clapping a repeated phrase either at the same time as the soloist or the first group or all the time. This latter provides an excellent start to group improvisation and the result would be on the following lines.

3

It is important to limit the length and help the shape, by saying that the soloist should make, say, four entries—it will surprise you how difficult the children will find it to stop at the correct time.

If we return now to our choral speaking with percussion additions built with the names of towns, we can proceed a stage further with our group improvisation. Let the children play the instruments as a background against which first of all you and then some children in turn improvise a simple melody on a suitable instrument.

When antiphonal work of this nature has been done it is easy to ask pairs or small groups of children to plan something entirely on their own, either of a similar form or an improvised melody accompanied by one or two rhythmic instruments. The players should be encouraged to experiment with the different instrumental combinations and also to make up rhythms and tunes appropriate to the instruments selected. It will be obvious that an accompaniment on a pair of cymbals would need to be less complex than one played on castanets.

26

All this group work is of tremendous value in helping the shyer children to express themselves. A leader in the class will often have retiring friends and will encourage them to support him in a group improvisation. Less bright children also find pure improvisation a great outlet for their emotions, especially as no written work is involved and they are able to play and work on more equal terms with their classmates. I recall the effect of a short weekly session of improvisation with a group of the lower stream, fourth year leavers in a secondary school. Many showed hidden talent and considerable skill with drums and the like and went to their next lesson having felt the joy of a constructive and cooperative period—it is a fact that the next teacher felt the benefit in increased willingness to work at their English.

Melodic improvisation in two part

THE PENTATONIC SCALE

Having acquired proficiency with three- or four-strand improvisation, we come to the problem of adding another melodic part—and this is where the value of the pentatonic scale becomes apparent. It is true that music can be improvised in parts in other scales, and it is desirable that attempts should be made in this direction, but it is usually more difficult and less immediately rewarding than part-playing in the pentatonic mode. This is due principally to the fact that intervals of a semitone never occur, but also to other more technical considerations such as the absence of a tritone, which occurs prominently between the fourth and seventh of the more common major scale. A glance at the example below will show a pentatonic scale based on the note C and the interval combinations.

As in modal music, any of the notes may be treated as the keynote or doh, and this is a further point making for easier improvisation, as less attention has to be given to harmonic progression.

If we return once more to our piece using town names we can

immediately make use of the pentatonic scale by singing or playing the town names on the 'cuckoo' interval of G and E instead of just playing them as rhythms and then, when this idea is going well, we can improvise a tune in the pentatonic scale on top. The result will be an exciting three- or four-part texture. It is usually best if at first you play the improvised part in order to give some idea of the possibilities. After this invite others to try; there will be plenty of offers. I find it better, when attempting new projects in parts, to take one of the parts myself for the first one or two runs. Children learn greatly by imitation and, if the point is not laboured, they quickly contribute their own individual and original approaches.

First exercises in two-part melodic improvisation are best limited to two or at the most three notes per part. By combining instruments of different pitch or quality the pupils appreciate more readily the advantage of the parts being independent in rhythm, with one having quicker notes at the moments the other has sustained notes. In the first example we will use two chime bars and a small glockenspiel which sounds an octave higher than the chimes and plays only three sounds.

In the second example we will try the effect of a pair of timpani and a descant recorder playing four notes. They will take it in turns to have quicker moving parts.

It is worth noting that although this example is pentatonic it is also clearly in a D minor mode and has a strong doh–soh bass.

Another facet of the use of the pentatonic (and one much beloved by the children) is the chance to play on the black notes only, which form a readily available five-note scale on keyboard and similar instruments. Classes appreciate nothing better than 'a trip to Java' (where our glockenspiels probably originated before finding their way to Germany), and a chance to make up a gamelan orchestra. Use as many chimes, glockenspiels, xylophones, gongs, shakers, cymbals, as possible and play in the pentatonic, either on the black notes if you have them or on C D E G and A if not. Bigger instruments have long notes, smaller ones move more rapidly—percussion add regularly spaced 'bongs' and 'clashes'. After their attempts, let them hear the real thing on a record.*

Occasionally, and if there are sufficient instruments, divide the whole class into groups and let each group work out and practise in different parts of the room, or the corridor if you dare, or the playground, weather permitting. Then have a class concert or even a competition, hearing each group in turn. This is one of the times when it is advisable to warn the teacher next door.

Chord improvisation

Turning now from the pentatonic, we come to another useful framework for improvisation: the chord. The broken form of the doh chord is the basis of many fine melodies and all bugle calls. The boys especially, but also the girls, will have great fun making up bugle call tunes. One of the best ways is to set out the three chime bars of the chord, say G B and D, with the possible addition later of lower D, and after demonstrating a tune or so yourself

* HMV, *History of Music in Sound*, Vol. 1.

invite a member of the class to make up a tune, preferably of a definite number of bars. Alternatively the glockenspiel or xylophone may be used with or without the unessential notes removed. These tunes may be answered, or extended, or combined with rhythmic percussion, or ostinato, or another chord melody in the same way as the pentatonic improvisations. The following example shows the idea.

As familiarity grows with the sound and feel of the doh chord tunes, two developments arise.

First, one of the players improvises a melody based on the notes of the tonic chord, but with neighbouring or passing notes as additional material, whilst the second player confines himself to the chord as before. This is a difficult step and should not be attempted until chord-based improvisation is fluent and even then a note added at a time should be the approach. A variation of the previous example would be:

The lower parts would be as before.

The second development is to introduce the notes of another chord, generally the dominant (or the dominant seventh). In this case chime bars are of great help as they can be set out in their chord groups and it then becomes an easy matter for the child to make up a tune by playing a bar or two on one group then switching to the other and then back to the first and so on.

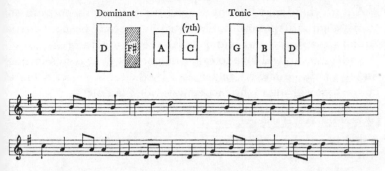

Tunes built in this way nearly always have a somewhat German or Austrian folksong flavour, especially the ones in three time which sound like the Ländler. However they are none the worse for that, providing in the process an effective antidote for too much of the rather harmonically static pentatonic mode and giving immediate and almost guaranteed satisfaction to the player and good harmonic aural foundations for the listeners. These ideas follow naturally from the suggestions made under 'Basic Chord Work' (Chapter 5) and they form a strong framework on which to build fine-sounding group improvisations, with chords on guitars, chimes and so on as additional support.

Improvisation round a dominant

An entirely free part circling round the dominant note (that is soh) and its immediate neighbours up and down may be added to any group improvisation built on the doh and soh chords. Pupils love to listen to the effect of their own melody first over one chord and then the other. An example is given below, but remember part 1 would be quite unhindered by harmonic considerations —these would only govern the lower parts by prior agreement.

31

A third chord may be considered desirable, but do not rush on to this stage until the possibilities of two chords have been explored. Although the bread-and-butter chords are the tonic and dominant, the adventurous will love to experiment with their own selection and this must be actively encouraged by the teacher—a few black chime bars will add to the excitement—for example

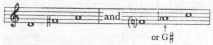

will give this:

All this improvisation is of inestimable value in approaching written composition and as soon as the simplest rhythms or tunes have been extemporized, a start should be made by attempting to notate something of a similar nature.

Free improvisation

When the foundations have been carefully laid and the players have enjoyed the support of a framework, they are then ready to swim in the unlimited ocean of sound and, because of the help they have received initially, will better be able to use purposefully the full gamut of the instruments of their choice.

An interesting and fruitful experiment I made with an unusually small group of nine children would follow suitably for pupils at this stage. The players were asked to group themselves in threes, each group having a melodic instrument, a bass (one timpano) and a pitchless percussion of their own choice. They were labelled A B and C and separated across the front of the classroom in distinct groups. The conductor's mission was to point, control and combine, as well as stop, with suitable signs, their group improvisations. This meant that any group might play separately, with another (A with B, B with C or A with C) or altogether. No prior discussion took place between the groups, but a common tempo was agreed at the outset, only interrupted when the conductor held both hands, palms facing the players, to indicate a silence. The resulting sound was musical, exciting and at times entrancing, despite the fact that they were entirely free to choose which notes they liked.

Finally a reference to musical illustration of stories or incidental music to plays must be made. This often proves a good way of stimulating the imagination of pupils who have few musical ideas. A story with several characters and a number of recurring situations provides the best material. Instruments are selected as appropriate and available, and it is often a useful occasion on which to split a scale of chime bars in an unusual way to give greater variety and further stretch the musical facilities. The story is told by the teacher or read by a child, and the instrumentalists provide suitable tunes or effects as their character appears or situation arises; this almost carries on the tradition of the Wagnerian use of Leitmotif.

Getting ready

Finally, I should like to make the following points about the preparations needed for any lesson that is to include instrumental work. In many classrooms the instruments will already have been set out in a music corner, but, if this is not so, attention to the ideas listed below will save valuable time in the lesson itself.

1　Have a table on which the instruments are arranged. *Or*
2　Leave the instruments stored methodically in a convenient cupboard, and allow the children to collect and return the instruments. They will soon realize the importance of returning them to their correct places, as they will not be keen to waste time looking for lost ones.
3　Whichever plan is adopted, make special provision for small items like beaters, which easily become lost if they are not returned to their own box or lodged inside the instrument, as in the case of glockenspiels etc.
4　Remember that the string instruments and the timpani require, as far as is possible, tuning in advance. It must be admitted that this is a slight disadvantage, as the teacher is often busy just before a lesson, but one which I hope will be outweighed by the additional colour and interest these instruments contribute to the lesson.

33

5 When instruments are given out, it is often better in the long run to do this by groups, allowing the children time to practise the newly issued instruments before proceeding to the next group. This depends to a certain extent on the work being practised, as sometimes, if a piece is being revised, it is more efficient to let the children collect their instruments as they come to the lesson and practise their own parts, as an orchestra does when tuning up.

6 Always insist that practice of parts ceases immediately you indicate that you are ready to proceed to the next stage. Be firm about this. It is better to withhold further issue, or withdraw the instruments for a lesson or two, until the pupils are prepared to respond to 'the tap of the conductor's baton'. This may seem unfair to those who do respond promptly, but this is a dilemma that all teachers are faced with; in my opinion it is essential that the class should understand this in order that worthwhile music making can proceed. In my experience, if it is necessary to take this action, once is usually sufficient, as their disappointment at not being able to play the instruments at one lesson, ensures that they cease practice more quickly when requested on future occasions.

7 Do not overlook the tremendous help that well-trained and willing monitors can give to the class. When the pattern of preparation is well established, monitors can most capably control the issue of instruments and, when necessary, music.

Do not forget that both improvisation and imitation, as with other techniques discussed in this book, will be only a part of any lesson and will take their place alongside the other musical activities, which must include singing. The material outlined in this chapter might span many years of a child's school life, and no attempt must be made to force the natural development of the creative ability. Instead the teacher can best provide careful guidance and sympathetic appreciation.

4
Ostinato

The dictionary defines the Italian word 'ostinato' as a ground bass
and refers one to 'obstinate' where we find: 'blindly or excessively
firm; unyielding; stubborn; not easily subdued or remedied;
persistent'. To us it will be interpreted as a note, notes, or phrase,
that recurs over and over again and which will normally be an
accompaniment to a melody. In its most organized form the
'basso ostinato' or ground bass is found in masterpieces like *Dido's
Lament* or the finale of the *St Anthony Chorale Variations* of Brahms.
In its most primitive form it would be a rhythmic phrase on a
tom-tom or the drone of a bagpipe. The drone makes a good point
of departure.

Traditionally the drone consists of doh and soh sounded together
and when performed by a bagpipe it is continuous. When other
instruments are used for the drone it is necessary rhythmically to
reiterate the sounds, either together

or one after the other.

It must be mentioned here, that although there are a large number
of melodies which sound effective with this type of accompaniment,
especially those that are pentatonic, those tunes with strongly
marked harmonic changes often sound forced when played over a
tonic-dominant pedal. For guidance a number of suitable nursery
rhymes are listed here.

> *Bobby Shafto*
> *Dickory Dickory Dock*
> *Oranges and Lemons* (change to lower drone for middle section)
> *Lucy Locket*

Over the Hills and Far Away
Polly Put the Kettle On
Little Boy Blue

If you or the class tire of the tonic dominant (doh–soh) drone, you may like to experiment with other combinations. At first they may appear strange, but gradually the fascination of new sounds will take hold of the class and you. One example will suffice to show the idea. Note a suitable tinge of sadness and dreaminess in the choice of notes.

Little Bo Peep

Because of its repetitive nature, an ostinato is easy and often exciting to play and is therefore most suitable for the simplest of instrumental accompaniments or two part pieces. Usually it will contain elements of the harmonic changes common to each bar and the following examples will help to make this clear.

Didn't my Lord deliver Daniel

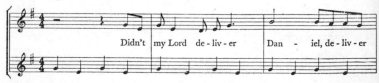

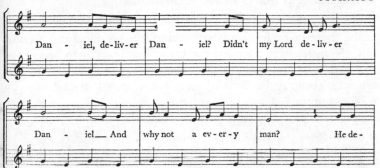

This is a very simple but completely satisfying ostinato which uses the drop of a third already found in the pentatonic melody. This may well grow to more elaborate versions such as the following, as control improves.

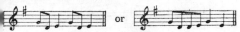

Masters in this hall

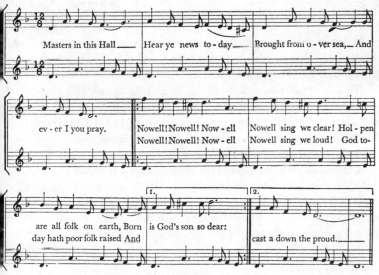

In the ostinato to this old French carol with words by William Morris care has been taken to imply both tonic and dominant chords and this helps it to follow the tune closely and harmoniously, there being few clashes except on the weaker beats. Notice that the ostinato is extended one extra bar in order to bring it to rest firmly on the tonic. This is usually better than leaving the ostinato abruptly in the air, and it is covered in this case by prolonging the last note of the tune.

The Campbells are comin'

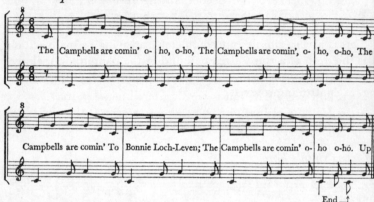

Again in this example the ostinato swings between doh and soh. The soh (in this case G) is decorated with the A above, which often provides a pleasing dissonance in character with the music. This G A G figure is derived from the tune which has this pattern of notes in bars 1, 3 and 5. Note that in this case the effect is more satisfactory if the tune is played an octave higher than it is written. In the last bar the tails down indicate a possible modification for the last appearance of the tune.

A useful shorthand device comes to mind whilst we are dealing with ostinati and that is the sign used in orchestral parts that indicates the repetition of the previous bar. The sign is easy to remember: ⁄. It should be introduced to the children at a suitable place in their musical education.

Rhythmic features

Study of the three previous examples will reveal some of the methods of arriving at an effective ostinato. Generally speaking if

38

the tune is pentatonic, any of the notes from that scale will provide material for the ostinato. When the most suitable sounds have been selected it only remains to cast them into a satisfactory rhythmic shape and this can often be arrived at by improvisation. If there is more time for study the following points deserve attention:

1   When a tune contains a great deal of quaver or other quick movement, keep the accompanying ostinato fairly simple, e.g. in *The Campbells are Comin'* the rhythm of the ostinato is a straightforward skip step which combines well with the quavers of the tune.
2   Where a tune has longer notes try to arrange the ostinato so that it moves on where the tune stands still. This is unlikely to work in every bar, but is worth attempting, e.g. in *Masters in this Hall* the ostinato has quicker movement at the end of the bars, whereas the tune often has longer notes on the second half of the bar.

Ostinati to major and minor tunes

In the case of major or minor scale melodies as opposed to pentatonic melodies, the best results will usually be achieved by remembering the rhythmic points stated above and then basing the ostinato round either the first degree of the scale, or the fifth, or both. Again we have the doh–soh of the drone.

Choosing an effective ostinato can make an interesting exercise for both teacher and class. Approach it in this manner.

1   Select the basic two or three notes for the ostinato.
2   Study the rhythm of the melody and decide on the most suitable rhythmic features for the ostinato.
3   Try each bar of the tune in turn with the ostinato and listen carefully to the overall effect.
4   Make modifications where necessary so that you arrive at the ostinato that will go best with the greatest number of bars.
5   Remember that the ostinato should remain unaltered throughout the piece, except at the end where a special termination is permissible.

This approach may seem mathematical and unmusical, but in practice it calls for real critical musical judgment. Some bars will inevitably have a feeling of tension, but this should relax as the music moves on. It is this tension and relaxation which gives the vital excitement not only to music with ostinati but to much other music as well.

Ostinati to rounds

Rounds, which are discussed more fully in the chapter on Basic Chords, often have regularly recurring tonic-dominant harmonies and therefore make most useful material for ostinato work. An example of this in a very simple form is provided by *London's Burning* where the first two bars may be repeated throughout as an ostinato.

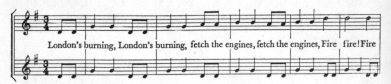

A variation to this is possible by combining bars 1 and 3 of the tune and using them as a two-part ostinato.

For greater rhythmic interest a switch in the rhythm of the ostinato will add considerably to the overall effect of the performance.

Note that any line of a round may be used as an ostinato whilst the other parts continue in the normal manner.

Ostinati as a background for improvisation

So far we have mentioned only the use of ostinati as accompaniments to tunes we wish to sing or play. We must also remember that an ostinato, whether played, spoken or sung, makes an admirable background against which a soloist can improvise. The ostinato helps in many ways but perhaps most of all by providing an impelling rhythm which steadily keeps the soloist going.

The pentatonic produces the most harmonious sounding combinations, but diatonic improvisations against a suitable 'ground' will prove most rewarding if the extemporizer listens as he plays and has already experienced the value of moving to doh at the end of his phrases. When plenty of basic practice has been had, even greater excitement will arise from more novel combinations of ostinati, with the use of the full chromatic range of the solo instruments.

Additive rhythms

As the ostinato is a primitive technique for group playing it gains tremendously from the vitality of complex additive rhythms of the kind found in African folk music. Pupils enjoy the challenge of trying to play such rhythmic ostinati as the following. They sound most effective when played on some form of hand drum, either a tom-tom or a tambour.

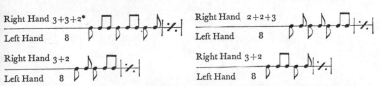

* The strange time signatures show the grouping of the quavers in the bar.

They may be performed on the same drum, using a variety of places for the attack, or on different drums, one for each hand. The soundbox of a guitar also is excellent for this type of rhythmical activity as each part of the body gives a different quality of sound when struck with the fingers. If none of these instruments is available play them on the desk or the knees.

4

Limitations of ostinato

Much of your best classroom instrumental work will almost certainly utilise the ostinato in some way, but it must be kept in mind that ostinati (however exciting) are by their very nature limiting in style and the teacher and class should advance to other musical forms of ensemble playing when they have experienced the pleasures to be gained from playing together. Ostinato will always have a place in classroom music, but do not let it be a 'cuckoo in the nest'. Even Purcell, who was a genius with the ground bass, used it less in his later works.

5

Basic Chord Work

This chapter is concerned with the kernel of much of our classroom instrumental work, as it is from the basic harmonies treated in this chapter that the structure of the more advanced ensembles is often built, while the same chords also provide all that is necessary in the way of harmony for the great majority of our song accompaniments.

There is nothing subtle in this chapter; it is strictly 'utility' and the more learned musicians may find the emphasis on root position primary chords almost crude. It is addressed principally to those who have had little or no training in harmony and tries to guide them through a few of the fundamental principles. When a class is reared on these same fundamentals, the pupils who proceed to more advanced work for G.C.E. and C.S.E. will not be in the position of approaching their harmony as if it were a mathematical construction; they really will know the sound and effect of the various chords.

Equipment

The chief ingredients required for this chapter consist of ten chime bars at a cost of about £7. When it is considered that so much practical music-making can take place for such a little outlay, the cost will seem small, especially if it is remembered that three or four long-playing records, for example, cost the same. More chime bars make possible a greater range of keys, but our first ten provide useful chords in several keys. To the chime bars any other instruments may be added as they become available. The following are particularly suitable for this purpose, as they supply a good bass: the timpani, 'cello (open strings) and of course the guitar,

43

which is treated more fully at the end of this chapter. It will be surprising these days if there is no pupil in the school who can lend a guitar to help out the poor music master or mistress, until they in turn are able to prevail on the headmaster to allocate £10 or so of the capitation allowance to buy one.

A tip must be added about the organization of the chime bars themselves. Unless you are lucky enough to have a boxed set, each chime bar will come, with its own rubber-headed beater, in a cardboard container. See that both box and lid are clearly labelled with the correct chime bar name (G, F♯ etc.) and then when preparing the lesson, leave the bars in the box with the lids arranged as in the following diagram, until you actually require to hand the chimes out, or let the children take them from the boxes. When the lesson is over, it is an easy matter for the last user of the instrument to return it to the correct box, *with its stick*, and close the lid.

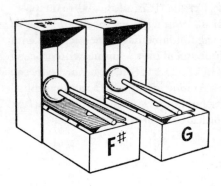

Chords

An enormous number of pieces can be accompanied by two or three chords (a few need only one). The three principal chords, in order of importance, are those based on the doh, soh and fah of the scale. The chords consist of three or sometimes four alternate notes of the scale, the lowest of which lends its name to the chord. So from the scale of G we derive our doh chord as follows.

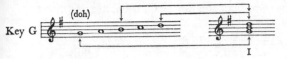

Key G

I

It is known as the tonic chord because the first note of the scale is the tonic, or I for short, or it might be referred to as the G chord because it is built on G.

Similarly we build a soh chord with alternate notes of the scale, but in this case on D which is the fifth note or soh in the scale of G. However to adjust it to a more natural vocal range and also to contain all the notes within the stave, we will use the lower D as our starting point.

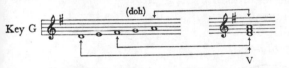

Key G

V

Frequently we find the soh or dominant chord has an extra note added to it, making four notes in all. This additional note is seven notes inclusive from the bass note D and the resulting chord is known as a dominant seventh. The dominant seventh is used extensively in simple folk songs and in most cases will be preferred when use of a soh chord is indicated. Notice that in the key of G both the soh chords have an F♯.

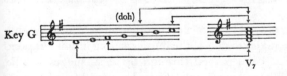

Key G

V_7

Lastly from one note further down the scale (C) we can build a fah or sub-dominant chord (IV).

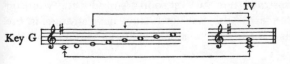

IV

Key G

Our three basic chords in the key of G, then, are as follows.

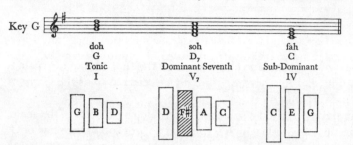

You will see that the note G occurs in both I and IV, so this makes it preferable to have ten chime bars C D E F♯ G A B C' D' and another G, in order that each group can be entirely independent.

Tonic or doh chord only

To start with we will confine ourselves to the key of G, as set out above and take a much loved round that will work quite pleasantly with the doh chord only.

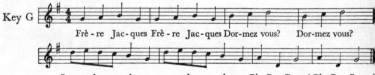

It may be sung or played by recorders or other melodic instruments and this applies equally to any of the music making in this chapter. Once the tune has been played through by itself, suggest to the class that a simple accompaniment might be a good idea.

1 Give out the chime bars G B and D to volunteers (there should be no shortage) and caution them not to play until requested.
2 Briefly demonstrate that the best sound is produced by letting the stick bounce off the bar and show how strange is the damped sound, if the beater is held stiffly in contact with the bar.

3 Next ask for the sounds to be played separately, starting with
   the lowest, so that the class can hear each constituent.
4 Now have the three sounds played together as a chord. Watch
   the class's delight. At first the chord may be untidy, and this is
   likely to be your fault if you have not counted them in or con-
   ducted them very clearly, but after a few more tries it will
   come together perfectly.
5 When the chord is precise, go straight on to adding it to the
   tune played or sung by the rest of the class. At first one chord
   to a bar will be easiest, then try two chords to the bar.
6 When all have tried this, go on to the following variations and
   appoint the player who has the lowest note, which in this
   chord is G, as the leader.

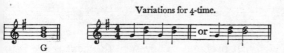

Variations for 4-time.

These alternative patterns add greater rhythmic interest and
vitality, as well as a clearer bass line. They will generally be
preferred as an accompaniment to the block chords that were
attempted first.

At this stage it will, in most classes, be a sensible idea to introduce
them to the notation for a chord and perhaps also to the variations
that you choose, as the notation gives a graphic representation of
the sounds. Whether they read the notes will depend on the stage
they have reached in their music-reading; the object of showing
the notation in this instance is to impress more clearly on their
minds the actual construction of the chord. Generally, when
writing music that is to be accompanied by this type of chord
playing, it is sufficient to write the melody and indicate the chords
underneath either by roman numerals or the letter names of the
roots of the chord, G, D etc. The pattern to be adopted might be
shown in one bar only. With a song, chord names might be added
above the appropriate word or syllable of the text.

Even if they do not read the notes from the stave, it will be a help
to the general organization of the class if they can early learn the
sounds that go to make up a particular chord, as this will enable

them to select quickly from a number of chime bars the particular bars they need for their purpose.

The next chord

In the round *Frère Jacques*, you and some of the class may take exception to the clash or dissonance occurring on the first beat of the last two bars. This is a matter of taste, but it will furnish us with a splendid reason for experimenting with another chord at this point. Try the next two examples, in order to see which of our other two chords sounds best with the tune in the last bars.

I expect most of you will prefer A. Therefore the next move is to divide the class into two groups, a doh chord group and a soh chord group, and to the latter allocate the chimes D F♯ A and C which is the chord used in example A above. Then perform the round again, but this time with the dominant seventh chord used on the first two beats of the last two bars. You will need to assist the entry of the dominant seventh chord and the return to the tonic chord by pointing clearly to the groups in charge of these chords. It is usually helpful if the chord groups coincide with the natural arrangement of the class, whether this be in rows or, as is more likely with the younger children, in table places. This assists the conductor to point without confusion to the chord required, which may not be so easy if the groups are not clearly defined. It is an easy matter to pass the instruments on to the next table or row when it is time for others to play. With these two chords many tunes may be harmonized, but a particularly good harvest of I and V tunes will be reaped from any book of rounds.

Selecting the chords : first method (by ear)

As few books mark which chords to use in the melody editions, and as also many of the accompaniments supplied for teachers to play to simple folk songs are often harmonically much too elaborate, we will discuss at this stage ways in which we can arrive at the correct chords to use with the melodies of our choice. As a first example we will examine *Michael Finnigin*, which is a great favourite over a wide age range.

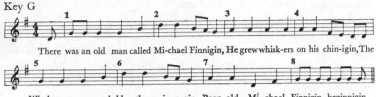

This tune is particularly suitable for playing on recorders because of its range, and on tuned percussion as well, as it has a good number of repeated notes; it is also most suitable for us at this point as it is effective if harmonized with the two chords I and V.

More often than not we can decide on the chords required purely by ear while we play the melody over, and this can become very good aural training by using the following process of trial and error. Write the melody on the board and number the bars, then have it played or sung and accompany it throughout with a doh chord on every bar.

The class will be most anxious to tell you that it does not fit very well in bars 3, 4, and 7. The next stage is immediately obvious. Play it again, but this time in bars 3, 4 and 7 try the dominant chord (i.e. D F♯ A and possibly add the seventh C*).

Notice that all the notes in bar 1 belong to the doh or tonic chord, but that in bar 2 there is an A which does not form part of the chord. This note is in an unimportant part of the bar on a weak beat and is known as a passing note, as it passes between one chord note and the next. Similarly in bar 4 the E is a passing note and can be disregarded from the harmonic aspect.

---

* With regard to the dominant chord, it is usually best to avoid the seventh when the chord comes right at the end of the phrase as at bar 4, but to include it when it comes just before the end of a phrase as at bar 7. To start with, this subtle differentiation is best overlooked, but, as skill grows and if and when the work progresses to a fully worked out arrangement, it may be kept in mind.

The complete harmonic plan for *Michael Finnigin* would be as follows:

Bars: 1   2   3   4   5   6   7   8
Chords: G G D D G G D$_7$ G

Lavender's Blue, which we will now harmonize, clearly demands the use of a chord other than I and V$_{(7)}$.

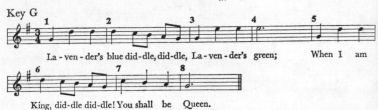

1   Play it through as before with a tonic chord to each bar.
2   Listen and note that the tonic chord is just right in bars 1, 2, 5, 6 and 8.
3   Now play it again but substitute the dominant chord in bars 3, 4 and 7.
4   It will be clear that it is only really suitable in bar 7.
5   Therefore in bars 3 and 4 use the sub-dominant or fah chord.

This will give us the following harmonies:

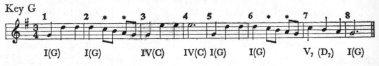

They will sound best if they are broken as in a waltz—*um cha cha*.

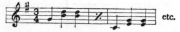

Notice the passing notes C and A asterisked in bars 2 and 6. As they occur on the first of two quavers on beats 2 and 3, they momentarily clash with the harmony of the bar and then move on to their resolution. Mozart made frequent use of this feature, which is known as an accented passing note, or appoggiatura.

One further point of interest arises in connection with the harmonic sequence for *Lavender's Blue*, and that is that it is very similar to the harmonic sequence used for a twelve-bar blues which is as follows.

I	I	I	I
IV	IV	I	I
V₇	V₇	I	I

Selecting the chords: second method

Two more examples must suffice, but this time we will change the key to C and also abandon the 'trial and error' method that we used with the class and assume that we are in the position of having no instrument to hand to prepare the harmonization. Therefore we must rely on our acquired knowledge, our previous experience and inner hearing. This is naturally much more difficult, and for most of our purposes the former method is the more useful; this outline of the second approach is added in order that you should gain a greater understanding of the theory behind the practice.

If we are to have the three primary chords I IV and V available in the key of C, we need to add the chime bar F natural to our collection, otherwise we will have to confine ourselves, when playing in this key, to tunes that require only the chords of I and V.

To assist our discussion here are the three chords I IV and V built on their respective notes of the scale of C. Notice there is now no sharp in the key signature.

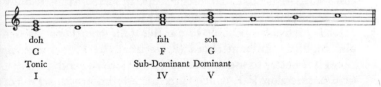

doh			fah	soh			
C			F	G			
Tonic			Sub-Dominant	Dominant			
I			IV	V			

(We deny ourselves the luxury of V₇ in the Key of C as it would require a top F bar as well as the lower F already needed for the sub-dominant chord.)

Notice that the two chords I and V are already familiar as they are identical with the C and G chords found in the key of G, but now they have a different function as the C chord will now sound final, as it is the tonic.

Below is the tune of *Jack and Jill*. We will look at it and deal with the points one by one.

Key C

1 Use one chord per bar and divide it as follows to define the two beats.

2 Examine the bars in turn and decide which bars are best harmonized with the tonic. Remember that the tonic chord may consist of any of the notes C E or G regardless of the octave in which they occur.

3 Bars 2, 4, 5 and 8 should be clearly tonic.

4 Bar 1 might be a problem as the note G occurs in both the tonic and dominant chords. In such a case as this, unless the tune starts on a half bar or up-beat, the first bar is usually best harmonized with the tonic chord.

5 In bar 7 it is also possible to use the tonic chord, but as this also fits the dominant chord (if we treat the E as a passing note) it is better to use that chord just before the end, to give a firm progression V-I, which is technically known as a Perfect Cadence.

6 Bar 3 has only the note D, which is part of the G chord, so this indicates the dominant chord.

7 Bar 6 similarly has only the note A, which is part of the F chord which in this key is the sub-dominant or IV.

The final version will have the following progression.

To dispel any idea that these simple harmonies are only suitable for nursery rhymes and are therefore accordingly for work exclusively with younger children, the next example is of rougher character.

Little Brown Jug presents few problems. Attempt a solution before reading the notes below.

Bar 1   Tonic
Bar 2   Sub-dominant
Bar 3   Mostly the note B, which is the middle note of the chord of G or Dominant. The lower neighbouring note A adds interest to the bar, but need not change the harmony.
Bar 4   C and E both belong to the tonic chord of C. The D is a passing note.
Bars 5, 6 and 7 are the same as bars 1 to 3.
Bar 8   The final bar: use a tonic chord; the D again is a decorating note that adds spice to the harmony.

Summary of three chords in four keys

Careful study of the five foregoing examples should reveal the elements of straightforward harmonization in the keys of C and G. Below are listed, for reference, tonic, sub-dominant and dominant chords in these and two other commonly found keys, along with the chime bars necessary for each key.

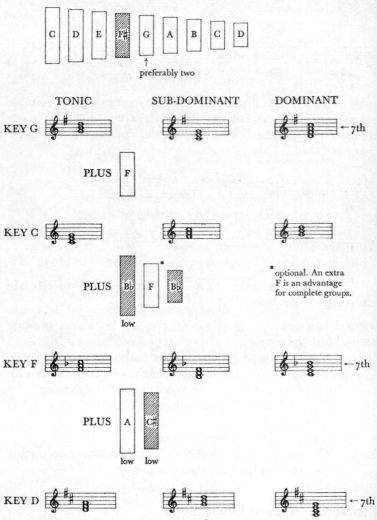

Minor and modal keys

In addition to the major keys listed, the same chime bars also provide satisfactory harmonies for some minor and modal keys.

It is not possible to deal with the subject at length in a book of this size, but you may like to try *O Rare Turpin* which uses only three chords which can be formed from our basic set of chime bars.

E minor D   G

What shall we do with a drunken sailor is another song which can be harmonized with just these two chords.

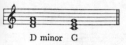

D minor C

Two special harmonic points

Before going on, it is necessary to mention two points that may appear to contradict what has been established earlier.

Occasionally you may observe that the second degree of the scale (ray) sounds well when harmonized with the sub-dominant chord, despite the fact that ray is not a part of that chord. This is especially so where the note, or group of notes, is followed closely by notes of the dominant chord. The chord that results from adding the supertonic (ray) to the sub-dominant (fah) chord is much used by Bach in his chorales and is known as the first inversion of the supertonic seventh (II_7b) and also as an 'added sixth'. Its name may worry you, but its sound will be quite familiar. Three brief examples should help to make the usage clear.

Christus, der ist mein Leben BACH

Last three chords in basic form.

y F

IV   V   I
(really II_7b)

55

One More River

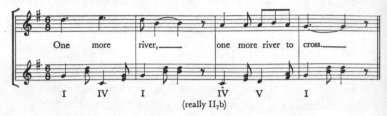

John Brown's Body

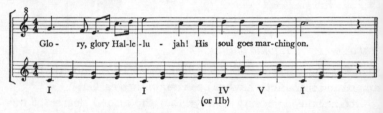

You will have noticed that all the above examples of II₇b occur near the end of a phrase.

Another phrase-ending frequently found, is the 'me ray doh' pattern that sounds like *Three Blind Mice*. This is usually satisfactory if harmonized with V–I. In this case the me, or third degree of the scale, is another example of an accented passing note or appoggiatura (mentioned when choosing chords for *Lavender's Blue*); it clashes momentarily against the chord before moving on to the note below, to become part of that chord. If this clash is found too harsh, try it with just the bass of the dominant chord and delay the other notes until the ray sounds. If this plan is adopted, greater harmonic clarity will be achieved by sounding the bass note again with the other notes of the chord, but this may not be considered necessary when working with chime bars as the bass note will sound on for quite a while until it is damped. For those who like the technical names, the first method, where the me sounds against the rest of the dominant chord, forms a dominant thirteenth (a popular chord at one period), and the second, where the me sounds only against the bass of the soh chord, is the bare outline of the progression known as Ic V. The 'c' refers to the inversion of the chord which is arrived at as follows.

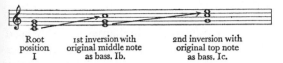

Root position I | 1st inversion with original middle note as bass. Ib. | 2nd inversion with original top note as bass. Ic.

Remember that this chord known as Ic is only really a decoration of V and therefore always moves on to $V_{(7)}$ when the decorative notes resolve. In fact it is only when we have a double set of decorating notes that the full chord of I can be seen, as in the following example.

Ib   IV   Ic   V   I

The 'E' and the 'C' in the third chord decorate the dominant chord and then move to 'D' and 'B' respectively in the fourth chord. By chance they form a chord of Ic in the process. If this seems very complicated, do not despair; it is included merely for those who like technicalities. Two examples follow to illustrate these points.

O Susanna (last phrase)

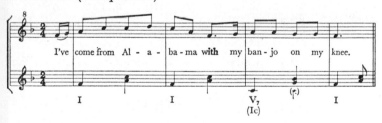

I've come from Al - a - ba - ma **with** my ban - jo on my knee.

I   I V_7 I
(Ic)

Three Blind Mice (last phrase)

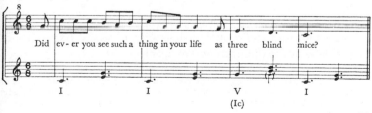

Did ev - er you see such a thing in your life   as three   blind   mice?

I   I   V   I
(Ic)

Bass instruments

All the suggestions so far mentioned in this chapter are improved by the addition of a bass instrument. This instrument may be a 'cello (or perhaps even a double bass in a lucky school), a home-made string bass, a viola or violin, a bass xylophone or alto metallophone, or a pair of school timpani. Even the lower and larger chime bars will add the extra resonance and depth that is so desirable when accompanying children's voices. The bass instrument plays in each case the lowest note of the chord in the octave most suitable to its compass.* This will usually consist of one note in the bar on the first beat. When the timpani is used, as there are only two drums, these are best tuned to the best sounding doh and soh of the key.

The following minuet adapted from Haydn's Symphony No 94 in G will show the various possibilities for our bass instruments.

The violin and 'cello open strings give us useful bass notes in several keys as the diagram will make clear.

* As teacher and class progress the bass can sometimes play one of the other notes of the chord when chord inversions are understood and greater melodic interest in the bass is needed.

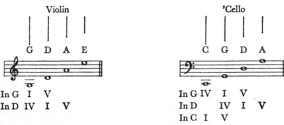

If, when using the timpani, the sub-dominant chord is required, the drum sounding the tonic note is used; as you will remember, the tonic note occurs in the sub-dominant chord. This was the practice followed in the classical orchestra and is illustrated by the following extract from near the beginning of Beethoven's First Symphony.

By the end of Beethoven's life a third drum had been introduced.

Chords on the Guitar

The guitar's open strings also provide useful bass notes for our chord work, sounding as they do, an octave lower than written.

However, if you possess a guitar I expect you and the class will wish to use it for chords as well. It is debatable which is the easier way to play the guitar for this purpose in the early stages. Most people naturally draw their thumb or fingers across all six strings and strum the instrument. This gives a pleasant sound, though somewhat lacking in rhythmic definition, but as it is difficult to by-pass a string it means that, in playing a chord, often six strings have to be accounted for and quite a number stopped with the left hand. If a plucking technique is tried with the right hand, it will be found to be only slightly more awkward, and it does mean that less strings need be stopped with the left-hand fingers. This is an important consideration when younger children, especially girls, are attempting the instrument. In addition this method gives greater rhythmic precision which is desirable in all but the dreamiest of lullabies.

Space only permits a brief introduction to the chords that we can play easily on the guitar and the following is offered as an aperitif rather than as a full course.

Position for holding the guitar

The first essential is to encourage the pupil to hold the instrument at an angle of about 45 degrees or slightly less from the horizontal, as this makes the left-hand technique a good deal easier. This can be done by resting the left foot on a small box about four to six inches high, although crossing the legs or resting the heel of the left foot against the chair leg also work and are fairly satisfactory for simple chord work.

Method of plucking

Remembering that the first string is highest in sound, but nearest the floor, ask the pupil to pluck the sixth string for his bass note, with the thumb. Then follow this by plucking the first three strings simultaneously with the index, middle and ring fingers on the third, second and first strings, respectively. When plucking the higher strings, the fingers should move towards the palm of the hand away from the thumb. Open strings plucked in this way will give the chord of E minor.

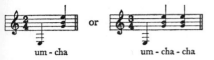

um - cha   um - cha - cha

Easiest keys for guitar playing

It is undeniable that the keys of E minor and E major are the most suitable to start with on the guitar as the tonic chords use a good number of open strings, but as these keys are rather out of our range for the other instruments we will move straight away to the chords that will be of use to us with other material from this chapter. For simplicity the chords are presented as chord diagrams or windows, with their staff equivalent underneath.* The fingers of the left hand are indicated above the diagrams with numbers (pianists should note that in common with all instruments other than the piano the number 1 stands for the index finger, 2 for the middle finger and so on). An 'O' means that the string is un-stopped, or open, and an 'X' that the string is not used. Always pluck the lowest sounding note for the bass with the thumb—it

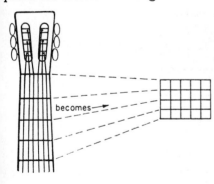

becomes

may be the sixth, fifth or, as in the chord of D major, the fourth string — and the higher strings altogether with the fingers. The most elementary chord pattern is used wherever possible, though more satisfactory versions of some chords are included and may be progressed to as skill increases.

Guitar chord diagrams

Key D (suggested first, because the move from the tonic to the dominant is simple)

* Each vertical line of the chord diagram represents a string, with first string on the right and each horizontal line represents a fret except the highest which represents the nut at the top of the finger board.

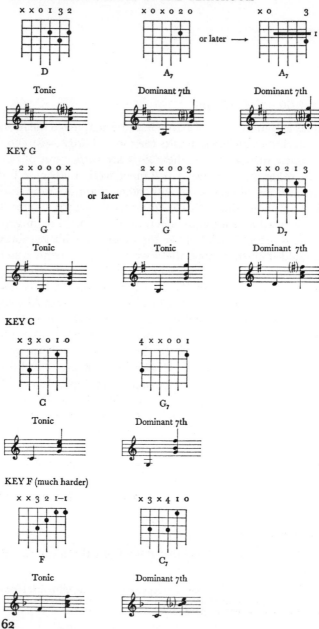

Only tonic and dominant chords are illustrated under each key, but it will be realized that the sub-dominant chord in D is the G chord and the sub-dominant chord in G is the C chord, and in C it is the F chord. It is unlikely that a child with only limited time in class to practise will be able to move freely between three chords in a key. In the early stages it is most convenient to have just one chord played with the tonic group. This will give the pupils time to become familiar with individual chord fingering patterns before attempting to move from one chord to another. If a second guitar is at hand this can be allocated to the dominant chord group and play with them.

This has been a long chapter and, for some, doubtless complex. But its mastery will enable you and your classes to come to grips with a harmonic language, which still dominates, rightly or wrongly, our musical environment. The addition of their own home-produced harmonies to songs and instrumental pieces will give children immense satisfaction and will be a valuable extension of their musical experience.

6

Song Accompaniments

Probably the most practical application of instrumental work is in the realm of accompaniments for songs performed in class. These accompaniments may be as simple as a quiet steady beat on a drum or, at the other extreme, quite elaborate instrumental textures. The song itself, coupled with the children's current instrumental skill, will dictate the most suitable choice for any one piece.

All the techniques treated in the last three chapters have their place in the accompanying of songs. Often a simple improvised rhythm will be all that is necessary; an ostinato may grow out of another song and provide an effective background; another may have well-defined harmonies and then a more chord-like treatment may be desirable. Any of these treatments may be combined and an outline melody based on the tune of the song added. This latter technique is particularly suitable in the early stages when the melody itself is too elaborate for the pupil's ability, whilst a simplified version helps the singers. It is also true that the less bright pupils often find a completely independent part difficult, but will happily play a line that fairly closely follows the tune they know.

As was mentioned in Chapter 1, the question of balance is of considerable importance. The instrumental accompaniment must never usurp the place of the singers, and care must be taken to limit the forces, especially the pure percussion. It is also worth stressing the value of any lower instruments we can secure, as these help enormously with the singers' intonation. Some children find greater difficulty in singing a melody when it is a bass line and all the other instruments are higher in pitch. This is often not surprising, as the melody does not always make a good bass. If no other lower instrument is available, set to and make a string bass with a tea-chest—it will be well worth the time spent.

64

Two further points need a mention before we go on to the examples of instrumental accompaniments.

Introductions

The first point is the value of an introduction to most songs. This is always better, even when accompanying the class yourself on the piano, and it is even more important when the accompaniment is provided by a group of pupils. The introduction should set the pace and establish the key (unless it is rhythmic only or the music is atonal). By having an introduction, you can give your undivided attention to the instrumentalists, before bringing in the singers. This gives everyone a chance to get things going properly and will assist the singers to make a confident entry. Introductions can consist of any of the following and are generally two or four bars in length, unless the phrase structure of the song is very irregular.

1 A basic beat.
2 A simple rhythm derived from the song.
3 A reiterated tonic chord or drone.
4 A tonic chord divided between instruments.
5 The first or last phrase of the melody.
6 The ostinato that is to be used for the song.
7 Any combination of the above.

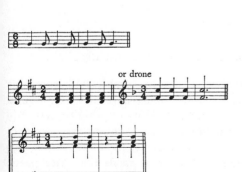

Choruses

The second point concerns the use of the chorus. Because the chorus is repetitive and often more 'catchy' than the verse and also because it is the natural place for everybody to sing or play, as opposed to just the soloist, it is a good idea in some songs to reserve the instrumental additions for the chorus and leave the verse unaccompanied. This method is particularly effective in songs that have a short chorus at the end of each line, as have many of those from the West Indies. In such cases the instrumentalists should be shown the manner in which a number of whole bar rests are collectively indicated, and encouraged not only to listen to or sing the verse, but also to count the bars rest as 123, 223, 323, 423 etc. in the case of three-time, or 1234, 2234, 3234 and so on in four-time.

Whole bar rest. Two-bar rest. Three-bar rest. Four-bar rest.

Eleven-bar rest.   Eleven-bar rest (more usually).

This is a good introduction to more complicated ensemble playing, where it is valuable to have some players silent for several bars at a time. Children always need plenty of practice, not only in counting whole bar rests, but also in counting the odd one- or two-beat rest that occurs in their parts. Again they find this easier if half their attention is directed towards the other parts, which will probably be continuing the beat in an audible manner.

We will now build up, as you might in class, accompaniments to four songs as illustrations of the foregoing remarks.

Clementine

First a very easy example with a strictly limited number of notes in the accompaniment. As there are many nursery rhymes and songs for younger children that lend themselves to simple treatment, I have selected a song that is more suitable for use with secondary pupils. It is frequently overlooked that many pupils arrive at secondary age having suffered many setbacks in a variety of subjects. Music is no exception and something can be done about winning them back to the subject if care is taken to choose activities that are immediately appealing and easily carried out, so that the children do not lose heart because of yet another failure. *Clementine*, which appears to be universally enjoyed, is a good song for this purpose as it is robust and harmonically straightforward, with a catchy and interesting rhythm.

Start by getting a rhythmic background under way. Clapping and slapping the knees will make a good basis. Sing the song through to these words, clapping and slapping at the same time.

Hands   knees hands, hands   knees hands, hands   knees hands, hands   knees hands

The third bar may prove tricky but the rest will help the actions. Then on an appropriate percussion instrument add the basic rhythmic feature of the song as an ostinato. When skill at handling the dotted rhythm develops it can be introduced on some other beat of the bar as a change from always coming on the third beat.

Once the 'rhythm section' is going well, introduce the melodic instruments. The tune for them suggested here uses only the notes D G and A, and these can be played on any suitable instruments from the tuned percussion, or on the open strings of a guitar, 'cello or violin. The outline of the melody is regular enough to teach by rote if this seems the best way, or even by writing the letter names like this: G | G D G | G D G | G D G | A D A, etc.

Accompaniment to 'London's Burning'

The final score to this round is presented on page 69. It should however be arrived at gradually, part by part, and a suggested order is indicated with numbers. Comments are added where appropriate. Whether the notation is shown fully to the players or, alternatively, in part only or not at all, is a matter for the teacher to decide according to the music-reading ability of the class, but such projects as a more complicated accompaniment to a song often afford just the stimulus required to further the interest in notation. The parts might be taught initially by rote and then the notation used as a prompt.

London's Burning

1st part. Might be played on two chime bars, the fourth and third open strings of a guitar, a xylophone, etc. Use two complete bars of it as an introduction.

2nd part. Chime bars in two groups play this. Note that they are omitted from the up-beat. The class and you might get used to the bar repeat sign.

3rd part. Recorders could play it as a round at two bars distance.

4th part. A percussion instrument on Fire fire! Triangle, Indian bells, Cymbal, or a 'D' chime bar.

5th part. 'Cello or string bass.

Remember that any part may be omitted and they may be introduced in any order. The song would still be enhanced and the children's participation increased if you could only manage instruments for the fourth part.

The German folk song *Ach, du lieber Augustin* is suitable for our next example. Again the parts might be added in any order you consider fit, or omitted altogether if the instruments are not available. The introduction could be melodic and derived from the tune as follows:

This has two features that are of value. The first is that, being a variation of the tune, it throws the song into relief when it comes, and the second is that it avoids top E, which is tricky to approach from D if a recorder is used. This is the type of outline tune that could double the voice all through, or perhaps join the singers in the last line only. Some may prefer to keep the lower D of the original tune.

After the introduction the accompaniment continues as follows.

Ach, du lieber Augustin

1st part. This is not quite an ostinato, but has an easily remembered pattern. It is easy to play on a glockenspiel or similar instrument as the repeated lower D in each bar can be played with the left stick, whilst the other notes are played with the right.

2nd part. Chime bars arranged in chord groups. Slight rhythmic variation adds interest.

3rd part. Divided between two percussion instruments, with plenty of rests to be counted.

4th part. Any bass instrument. Notice the extra movement in the bars just before the end of the phrases.

In addition the last phrase might be accompanied with clapping and slapping.

In the two previous examples and in any arrangements where chimes are used, more advanced figurations may be attempted as the skill of the groups improve. The following examples show possible developments of a G chord in two- and three-time.

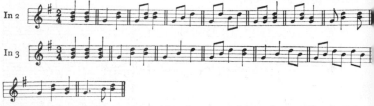

To finish we take an example of a song with a chorus, the exciting Jamaican folk song *Ball Gawn Roun'*.

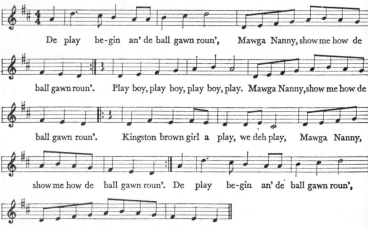

As the song is a fast one, many children may find the quavers in the chorus difficult on an instrument. The chorus comes at the end of each line and as lines 1 and 3 are repeated this makes six appearances in all. The following parts can be added to the singers one at a time, until there is a wonderful conglomeration for the sixth time.

Tune
1 Simplified outline: use recorders or pitch percussion.
2 Contrary motion tune for a good player. There are usually a few in any class.
3 Two-note part for chimes, xylophone or recorders.
4 Scraper or other percussion.
5 Another two-note tune which could be an octave lower.
6 Off-beat pizzicato violin open strings.
7 Any bass instrument.

Mawga Nanny, show me how de ball gawn roun'.

Further interest can be added by asking some members of the class to improvise a suitably syncopated rhythm, or background of off-beat clapping.

6

7

Group Ensembles

When we come to purely instrumental music, we are immediately faced with the problem that the music we choose or compose must have a melody that the pupils can play on the instruments we have at hand; we cannot rely on the voice to furnish the melody and the instruments the accompaniment only.

If we have in our class very capable children who have learnt the recorder for some time or play a violin, a wide range of music is possible; many country dance tunes sound admirable when treated in the ways outlined under previous headings. On the other hand, if the music-making ability is limited to the knowledge the pupils have acquired in class, we have to take care in selection of suitable tunes for instrumental treatment. As one of our fundamental points, stated in the first chapter, was that most of the music should be capable of achievement with skills practised during the lesson, we will take as our examples the simpler type of tune and leave the Irish jigs and so forth to those who are lucky enough to have pupils whose technique rises to these heights. However, in addition to the straightforward improvised, ostinato or basic chord treatment, which will be readily usable by classes with very elementary knowledge, we will add a section at the end of this chapter on the arranging of small instrumental pieces drawn from a variety of composers.

When planning an example in group ensemble work we need not exclude the possibility of an instrumental version of a song melody and so for the first example we take the five-note German folk song, which is almost the recorder's signature tune!

German folk song

As in many simple instrumental pieces the only notation that need be given to the children is the melody; the rest can be indicated by chord names, or left to the improvising ability of the performers. This tune can be played by any of the melodic instruments as it presents neither rhythmic nor melodic problems. The harmonies, too, should be clear if what was learnt in Chapter 5 is applied, but there is one catch in bars 7 and 15. These bars look like tonic harmony, but sound best if treated like the *Three Blind Mice* passage, that is by using only the bass note of the dominant chord against the first pair of quavers and the rest of the chord on the second beat, which implies the harmonies Ic V_7. Our complete harmonic scheme should be as follows with one chord to a bar.

Key G

G	D_7	G	G
G	D_7	D_7	G
D_7	D_7	G	G
G	D_7	D_7	G

Having established these basic harmonies, the next step may be:

1 Melody on recorders, glockenspiel etc.
2 Basic chords on chimes or guitar, um-cha, or umcha-cha pattern.

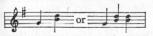

3 Bass of the basic chords on 'cello, timps, etc. tuned to G and D.
4 An improvised percussion part, perhaps on two instruments, keeping the rhythm moving where the melody has longer notes.
5 A second melodic part for more capable recorder or tuned percussion players, which would need to be notated.

This second part should use mostly the notes from the chords for each bar, but not as a rule those being played by the first part at the same time. Although the following example is of an extra underneath part, the new part can equally well lie above the tune, in which case it functions as a descant.

75

Notice that the tails of the tune all go up and those of the second part down. This second part is confined to just the notes of the chords, but some may prefer to add non-chord passing notes at certain places, as in the third line.

'Nancy's Fancy' : an English folk dance

For our second example we will arrange the English folk dance *Nancy's Fancy*. Further development of the same idea might provide useful home-produced music for the school dance teams.

We will assume that in this instance we have no chimes or guitars for our basic harmonies, although naturally this tune sounds well with them. Instead we will add easy parts for a second less advanced recorder, a xylophone, an open string violin and a drum. These, with the exception of the drum, will give us the harmonies we require. The tune should be rehearsed first and needs plenty of practice as it is a quick one. Slurs have been included in the tune as these add to the effect of the performance. In recorder music the slurs indicate that the first note only should be tongued. When the tune is going well, the other parts may then be added in the order suggested by the numbers in brackets.

Instrumentation of short keyboard pieces

So far the pieces we have dealt with have been folk or traditional melodies where a certain flexibility in the harmonies used is acceptable. When we come to orchestrate small compositions for our mixed groups, it is only reasonable that we adhere as far as is possible to the harmonies used and implied by the composer, otherwise the piece becomes distorted in character and inartistic in effect. All we can do is to adapt the original parts to the needs of our forces and where necessary thicken the texture with additional parts that blend with the prevailing harmony, often more clearly defining it in the process. A little thought should show us

77

that the latter is no great 'sin' where the seventeenth and eighteenth centuries are concerned, as the harpsichord continuo player did just this by filling out the harmonies between the contrapuntal parts.

Sonatina movement

The Sonatina School often furnishes useful material for arrangement and the first extract is by L. Köhler, who lived in the middle of the nineteenth century. It is the first theme of the Rondo from a sonatina in G.

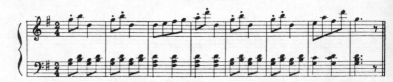

This theme could be reduced to the basic chords I, IV and V, but in this case our arrangement needs to be written out in full for the class as the chords do not occur in the root position form only. Because of this, the students will need to read the musical notation, especially if later you decide to instrument the whole movement.

The melody covers a range of an octave and is easily playable by recorders or pitch percussion. It will need to be notated an octave lower than it is in the piano score, but you will recall that descant recorders and many pitch percussion instruments sound an octave higher than written and so the resulting sound will be at the correct pitch.

Looking now at the left-hand part, we have to face the fact that we may have to transpose this up, as we have few instruments that are able to reach these lower notes. The G is no problem, as it is available on violins, guitars and very low chimes, but the F sharp is less readily accessible. We may have to make a compromise and alter the chords in the third and fourth bars so that D is their lowest note, or perhaps add just the bass line on the piano and leave the quaver movement to the xylophone.

Our score is now complete in all essentials, but other instruments and players can be gainfully employed filling in some inner parts and adding a light percussion accompaniment. A completed score might take the following form, which includes a piano part that is considerably more interesting without being very much more difficult to play.

If an arrangement of the whole movement was envisaged, it would be better to save some instruments for a later section, or alternatively start with them all and then omit some at a later point in the movement.

Piece by Jeremiah Clarke

The well-known Trumpet Voluntary, once attributed to Purcell, was originally a harpsichord piece known as *The Prince of Denmark's March* and composed by Jeremiah Clarke. It sounds quite fascinating on our types of instruments.

As the melody lies rather high for recorders, necessitating the extensive use of 'pinched' notes, we will allocate it to the dulcimer or small glockenspiel, which sounds two octaves higher than written. This will allow the large glockenspiel or xylophone to play the lower part one octave higher than it appears in the keyboard music, and its melodic quality is thus preserved. The bass may be doubled on certain notes with a string bass, 'cello or timpani on D and A and some inner parts could be added to give greater fullness. The completed score would be like this.

Arrangements of this nature may offend your taste, in which case it may be best to keep to simpler material, but before dismissing them too peremptorily consider how much more flexible was the composer in his choice of instruments before the standardization of the modern symphony orchestra occurred in the nineteenth century, and try also to imagine such a piece as the Jeremiah Clarke played on the higher register of an organ. At times a xylophone with its liquid tone produced with soft felt hammers sounds not unlike an organ. Also consider the true appreciation that will result from really 'getting inside' a composition by these means.

81

Original composition

The other solution to instrumental music is to write specially for the instruments. This activity will grow quite spontaneously from the children if they are given encouragement with their improvisation, ostinato and chord-playing. The subject is too great to deal with at length in this book, but a start can be made with notating their own rhythms and simple melodies (often helped by setting words) and to these add ostinato and chord accompaniments. The need to write and record on paper their creative music-making will be yet another stimulus to encourage their musical literacy.

8

Notation and Instrumental Games

The activities outlined in the foregoing chapters will do much to arouse the desire to make music in more advanced ways, and pupils will be stimulated to gain more knowledge about their instruments and also to become more musically literate. It is to be hoped that from these simple and enjoyable instrumental beginnings each child will early realize the pleasure to be gained from playing an instrument in the company of others, and will be encouraged in every way to pursue a more detailed study of a particular instrument as an out-of-class activity. This study will be assisted by the fact that at some stage in our music-making the need to become familiar with notation will have arisen and been satisfied, and also because our class music-making will have greatly developed the pupil's aural sense.

It must be left to the individual teacher to decide when the time is ripe for attention to be given to notation. It may be early or late, but should always grow out of the work in hand and is often best introduced by notating a phrase which has already been learnt by ear, rather than by the more usual but unrealistic approach of learning the notes and then working out the tune. The former method is akin to showing a child how a word which he already has in his spoken vocabulary looks on paper—this is natural and logical and can be adapted to the method of teaching music-reading, which is incidentally much more systematic than our English spelling. This approach of listening before reading is now widely accepted as the best method of learning a foreign language, especially in the primary school. A child's need to write down the music often grows from a desire to record his own musical creation and this provides a powerful incentive to master the craft of notation.

Notation of rhythm

In my experience, the best method of teaching rhythmic reading is with the help of the French time names, which give an immediate verbal representation of the time pattern and are entirely systematic. Some of the rhythmic imitation work suggested earlier might well include some work with time names. A simple rhythm

♩ ♫ | ♫ ♩ | could be clapped and the children asked to

time name back the rhythm instead of clapping, Ta ta-te | ta-te ta, and so on.

Below are listed the basic time names with a crotchet in simple time and a dotted crotchet in compound time as the beat.

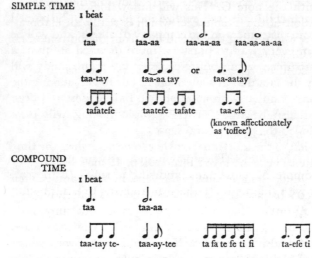

After this their complexity may be considered to outweigh their usefulness, but by this stage a firm grasp of rhythmic patterns will have been achieved.

Notation of pitch

By careful choice of material for instrumental work the range of notes recognizable from staff can gradually be increased.

It is to be hoped that some of this staff-reading ability may grow from previously gained knowledge of sol-fa applied to staff notation. If so, it is usually an easy matter to start to use pitch names which are constant, instead of the sol-fa names, which present the slight difficulty of doh being on any line or space. This is in no way a denigration of the sol-fa method, which in my opinion is invaluable in teaching young children a sense of relative pitch and the ability to sing at sight.

But our concern here is with staff notation for instrumental playing, and the following plan, which I always found successful in class teaching, should be of assistance. Always remember that it must be related to and should arise naturally from the instrumental work being attempted at a particular time. Its time scale will vary from months to years—do not rush it.

1. Start with the note G. This will follow logically from an explanation of the Treble Clef which is really an elaborate cursive *G* establishing the second line from the bottom of the stave as G.

2. Let the children time name a rhythm and then say it to the name G.

G G G G (ee) (ee) G G G G G (ee)

3. Sing it on the note G. Then play it on an instrument.

4. Add the note A. Time name and sing to sol-fa (if they are familiar with this method), then say and sing to latter names. Then play it.

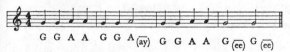

G G A A G G A (ay) G G A A G (ee) G (ee)

5. Add the note B. Time name and sol-fa, then say and sing to letter names. Then play it.

B A G (ee) A B G (ee)

(These first five steps will usually take only a little time, but when step 5 is reached much practice will be necessary.)

85

6   In a similar manner add C and D.

(With many classes these five notes G–D will prove quite sufficient for a term's work; with some children, much longer.)

7   Then work down the scale using at first F sharp. Some explanation will be necessary for F sharp and the key of G. Ask the class to listen to the effect of a well-known tune like the National Anthem or *Bobby Shafto* played with doh as G, but with an F natural. They will soon realize the need for the 'black note'.

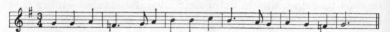

(By the way, this tune is the best I know for teaching the awkward rhythm ♩．♪ .)

8   Lower D and E. They will like singing *There's a Hole in my Bucket* to letter names. (Do not let the children try to fit-in the words 'lower D' or 'F sharp' as this spoils the rhythmic flow. However they must remind themselves mentally of these qualifications.)

7a and 8a   Alternatively the note lower D might be taught first (especially if using recorders, where the correct fingering is assisted by using this order) and followed by E and F sharp.

9   Middle C and the key of C come next. Londoners are helped to remember this by reference to the London Transport sign ⊖.

10 F natural for use in the key C.

11 At this stage, we have nearly all the notes within the stave. Now is the time and *not before* to present the idea of a 'ready reckoner'. Not many pupils in fact need it, but some will find it helpful. I refer to the well-known *Every Good Boy Deserves Favours* (which has strange moral values) or *Eat Good Bread Dear Father* (which is pleasantly reminiscent of the nineteenth

century) and of course F A C E for the spaces. The latter cannot be bettered, but for the lines I found the following more acceptable—the boys in the secondary school adopted the first most readily.

(Boys)

Engine Goes By Diesel Fuel

(Girls)

Every Girl Buys Dainty* Frocks

* Secondary girls prefer 'dashing'; the boys of the class thought 'dopey' more appropriate!

If you do not care for these use the good old favourites or make up your own. Better still, hold a class competition and award a prize for the best suggestion. Children always enjoy games and competitions and I see no harm in using this for musical purposes.

Musical games

The following musical games should add extra zest to the repetition and revision work usually needed to master the notation of music, and most of them provide valuable ear training as well. They are not a substitute for a carefully planned 'build-up' of music-reading ability, but do provide a pleasant change from more normal approaches. It will be found that the team games in particular greatly stimulate those pupils who have shown a certain indifference to becoming musically literate. There always seem to be a few of these in any class, however exciting the music-making has been and the 'disgrace' of letting down their team often proves to be just the incentive they need.

The games are not presented in a particular order and the degree of difficulty can be adapted to the requirements of the class.

1 MUSIC READING ON CHIME BARS
  DISTRIBUTED ONE NOTE TO A CHILD

A tune is written on the board and the bars handed round the class. Sometimes as each bar is taken out of its case, it can be

87

sounded and compared with its doh; the pupil who can give its sound correctly may have the chime. (Naturally this cannot be the procedure every time, as it would probably mean in most classes that the children requiring most practice would be delayed in having a turn because they would have been unable to recognize the sound.) When all the necessary notes are out, count at a steady pace and start the performance. It demands a good degree of careful listening on the part of each player to judge exactly when to strike the chime. This is especially so where quavers or long notes have to be taken into consideration and because of this the first attempts should be very straightforward rhythmically. The result is quite stereophonic (as the sounds come from all parts of the class) and always excites interest. When the first set of players have performed, they can each pass their chime bar to their neighbour and the performance is repeated, or another tune played.

2 A TEAM GAME VARIATION OF CHIME BARS ROUND THE CLASS

Using a method similar to the above, a team game variation can be played by having a series of tunes of the same range reproduced on sheets, which are distributed to all members of the class. Then divide the class into teams of eight (or however many notes of the scale are to be included) and arrange the bars along the front of the class. Each team comes out in turn and when its members are assembled, announce the number of the tune they are to play. By delaying the announcement of the number until this point, collusion is prevented. Mark the efforts out of five and total up at the end of a certain time. This competition gives a great deal of reading practice, as all the members of the class follow keenly the performances of each team. If they are not able to see who has played, it gives valuable ear training as well.

3 INDIVIDUAL READING OF SHORT PHRASES

This is a good way to help with a particular instrument as well as with musical notation. Again it is played with even greater keenness if the children are grouped in teams. Write about ten phrases of approximately equal difficulty and length on the board and ask each member of the team to play one in turn; award marks and total at the end. By having a few examples not too noticeably easier than others, one is able to assist less able readers. If the class had recently been practising the first five notes of the recorder, the following might be written on the board.

* Repeated notes give surprising trouble.

4 IMITATION OF PHRASES

(a) Rhythmic—as outlined in Chapter 3.

(b) Melodic. Limit the notes and set out chimes and so forth in such a way that there are two sets in positions where the contestants cannot see what each other are playing. The first plays a phrase and the second plays it back.

If the notes are limited to two, surprising effects can be produced between timpani and chimes, or open strings on a 'cello or guitar. This game is excellent aural training, but it is important to progress very steadily, adding a note at a time. When there are several notes the slower and less gifted (aurally) will find it too difficult. Again it may be played on a team basis.

5 RECOGNITION OF PHRASES

A number of phrases are put on the board or reproduced beforehand on paper. A child is asked to select and play one. The other members of the class have to guess which was played. The one who guesses correctly may come out next, or alternatively it may be played as a team game. The need for accuracy in music-reading becomes very clear both to each player and the rest of the class.

6 MISTAKE SPOTTING

Children love the deliberate mistake. Put a melody on the board and number the bars. Play it and include one alteration. The spotter must say which bar and beat and, if possible, which note was played instead. If you like, the alteration may then be notated and another 'mistake' made when the tune is played again. If this is done several times the tune may be changed completely. Once you have shown the way, it is then an easy matter for the pupils to set the problem.

In conclusion

Finally remember these points:

Music is for enjoyment and enrichment.

If it is enjoyed many other benefits follow.

Music is generally enjoyed most as a social activity.

Instrumental group work is one branch of this activity; do not forget that singing is another.

There are two aspects of musical art, creative and recreative: both should be developed. Some children will excel as 'composers' and improvisers, others will contribute most and derive most pleasure from performing. Many will be equally at home in either.

The material outlined in this book is of great value in developing a delight in solo and collective music-making. It is to be hoped that as a result of this class activity many children will pursue music more fully in other ways, and that all will carry their delight and appreciation of music over into the increasing leisure time of their adulthood.

Appendix A

Suitable songs for instrumental work drawn from books in wide use in schools, six useful carols and six nursery rhymes

For simplicity songs have been quoted only where they appear in a book in a suitable key; many more from the same books would be suitable if they were transposed up or down into easier keys (e.g. E♭ down a semitone to D, or E up a semitone to F). Only about six songs have been selected from each book; in some books many more are as useful.

1	*The Club Song Book for Boys*	(Boosey & Hawkes)
2	*The Club Song Book for Girls*	(Boosey & Hawkes)
3	*Collected Folk Songs*, Vol. 1	(Novello)
4	*English Folk Songs for Schools*	(Curwen)
5	*A European Folk Song Book*	(Arnold)
6	*The National Song Book*	(Boosey & Hawkes)
7	*Oxford School Music Book*, Beginners Book 1	(O.U.P.)
8	*Oxford School Music Book*, Junior Book 1	(O.U.P.)
9	*Oxford School Music Book*, Senior Preliminary	(O.U.P.)
10	*Rounds from Many Countries*	(Chappell)
11	*Sing Care Away*, Book 1	(Novello)
12	*Something to Sing*	(Cambridge)
13	*Songs for Juniors*	(Schofield & Sims)
14	*The Song Tree*	(Curwen)
15	*Fifty Songs for Schools*	(Associated Board)
16	*Six useful Carols from various sources*	
17	*Six useful Nursery Rhymes from various sources*	

N.B. In all cases the chord suggestions have been kept basic. More adventurous or more advanced classes and teachers would be well advised to attempt their own harmonizations and compare the effectiveness of the different versions.

1. *The Club Song Book for Boys*

Wiseman and Northcote (Boosey & Hawkes)

Down in Demerara

(2 chords F and C_7. Easy melody for glockenspiels etc.)

Polly Wolly Doodle

(2 chords F and C_7. Rhythmic interpolations in chorus.)

Hauling on the Bowline

(Good for instrumental participation in chorus,
outline melody if B♭ available + percussion.)

Old Zip Coon

(3 chords D, A_7 and G.)

The Lone Star Trail

(1 chord of G. Pentatonic melody, so improvisation on any
of the notes G A B D E possible. Easy melody to play
except top E for recorders.)

Shepherds Shake off Your Drowsy Sleep

(Drone on D and A.)

Border Ballad

(Drums for rhythm.)

2. *The Club Song Book for Girls*

Wiseman and Northcote (Boosey & Hawkes)

One More River

(2 chords F and C if you do not mind all tonic harmony in
bars 9 and 13 of tune. Use C bass and then the chord in
bars 3, 7 and 15.)

Cockles and Mussels

(Easy tune G–D plus lower D, suits recorders etc. Rhythm
may cause trouble at first. 2 chords G and D_7.)

The Orchestra

(Active rhythmic participation possible. 3 chords in D, fairly
easy with guitars.)

I Know Where I'm Goin'

(Easy with 2 chords, but is very fine unaccompanied.)

The Cockle Gatherer

(Again delightful unaccompanied, but can be performed with
very light *ad lib* percussion.)

3. *Collected Folk Songs*, Vol. 1
Sharp and Vaughan Williams (Novello)

(Many of the songs in this collection, like so many English folk songs, are better sung unaccompanied.)

Dashing away with a Smoothing Iron
(3 chords in G. Use D₇ in second whole bar and at similar places throughout.)

Heave Away, my Johnny
(Chorus could have a basic A | A A | A A | E E | A pattern, or with 5ths on these notes.)

I will Give my Love an Apple
(Add a drone of A and E sounded once per bar.)

One Man shall Mow my Meadow
(Ostinato from 1st two notes of song.)

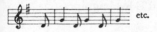

The Keys of Canterbury
(5-note tune E–B. Harmonize with E minor and D minor, 1 chord per bar except penultimate.)

4. *English Folk Songs for Schools*
Gould and Sharp (Curwen)

Henry Martin (2nd version)
(Drone on D and A—appropriate to words.)

High Germany
(Rhythmic improvisation, perhaps 2 players.)

Strawberry Fair
(3-note chime bar part on G, A and lower D is effective, but the changes are irregular—start with

use A and D in bars 8–11 of tune.)

The Old Woman and the Pedlar
(Outline tune omitting off-beat quavers, i.e. the E and G in 1st bar. Substitute A for C sharp if latter not available.)

Cock a Doodle Do
    (1 chord—the guitar's favourite E.)

5. *A European Folk Song Book*
   Horton (Arnold)

The Bee Swarm
    (2 chords G and D$_7$. Use D$_7$ in bars 4 and 7 of tune.
    Percussion might be used for bee-noises.)
Water-Wagtail
    (Easy tune except for top E for recorders. 2 or 3 chords.
    Light percussion accompaniment, perhaps a triangle.
    An underpart a third lower might be added except where
    tune has G.)
I would Wed a Tailor Bold
    (2 chords G and D$_7$, or a drone G and D for bagpipes.)
Lullaby
    (Pentatonic—improvise on E G A B or decide on an ostinato
    from these notes.)
With the Fife and Bagpipe too
    (Drone on D and A—possibly changing to G and D in middle
    where tune is repeated higher (bar 11) and then returning
    (bar 17). Similarly on repeat. Might be possible to add the
    fife effect in places with a recorder. Drum could improvise.)
The Cuckoo
    (2 chords G and D$_7$, or single chimes on these notes.)

6. *The National Song Book*
   Stanford and Shaw (Boosey & Hawkes)

    (Many of these books in schools although only a small
    percentage of the songs effective with simple accompaniments.)
Begone Dull Care
    (2 chords G and D$_7$, mostly occurring in each bar, except
    'Long time ago' etc.)
Barbara Allen
    (3 chords D, A$_7$ and G. A counter melody improvised on
    chimes grouped in chords would be effective.)

The British Grenadiers
   (3 chords G, D₇ and C. Mostly G, but use D₇ on the scale
   just before the end of 1st and 2nd phrases. Free percussion.)
The Campbells are Comin'
   (Ostinato mostly on C and G.)
My Love's an Arbutus
   (Try a G and D drone for 1st and last phrases and a D and A
   for 2nd and 3rd.)
Darby Kelly
   (3 chords G, D₇ and C.)

7. *Oxford School Music Book*, Beginner's Book 1
   Reynolds (Oxford University Press)

Hey Jim Along
   (Pentatonic, use any of the notes G A B D E for ostinato or
   improvisation. 1st bar repeated at beginning of each line
   might be given to chimes, but simplify rhythm to ♩ ♩ ♩ ♩
   or even ♩ ♩ ♩)
Ten in a Bed
   (1 chord G.)
The Neighbours
   (Use outline melody G A D B 4 times over on chimes.
   Add lower part G D₁ D₁ G.)
I'm a Little Drummer
   (*Ad lib.* rhythmic work. Encourage some rhythmic movement
   when melody has rest.)

8. *Oxford School Music Book*, Junior Book 1
   Fiske and Dobbs (Oxford University Press)

Bobby Shafto
   (2 chords G and D₇.)
Down in Demerara
   (2 chords G and D₇. Easy repetitive tune to play on chimes.
   Improvise part round note D.)
Michael Finnigin
   (2 chords G and D₇. Extra percussion suitable. Outline tune
   omitting off-beat quavers.)

Turn the Glasses Over
(Pentatonic, improvise on any of G A B D E. Keep things going on 2-beat notes. Alternatively work out suitable ostinato.)

Little John
(2 chords—easy tune.)

Hush-a-bye Darling
(Fairly easy tune. 3 chords G, D₇ and C for last line first 2 bars.)

Long Chain
(Good for starting with 1 chord D, although an A₇ in bars 6 and 13 would be better.)

9. *Oxford School Music Book*, Senior Preliminary
Fiske and Dobbs (Oxford University Press)

(Some very useful recorder pieces throughout the book will adapt well for use with other instruments.)

The Wishing Well
(A good start for guitarists—1 chord E.)

The Camelshair Cap
(1 chord G or 2 chords G and D₇. Outline tune with simplified rhythm to avoid some of the repeated notes. Make up second parts on the notes G, B and D.)

The Little Butcher
(Except for third line, easy tune for most instruments. 2 chords G and D₇.)

The Locked Door
(2 chords D and A₇. Use improvised rhythm for accompaniment as well.)

If I could Choose
(Good German folk song for use with 3 chords. A descant can be developed by playing the tune a third higher and modifying the part where necessary.)

Ball Gawn Roun'
(Chorus on instruments.)

10. *Rounds from Many Countries*
Anderson (Chappell)

Ho there Punchinello
(Chord pattern ‖: F | C$_7$ C$_7$ | F :‖)
Sing, Sing Together
(Chime the last line over and over again as an ostinato.)
Doctor Fell
(Easy tune, use on different instruments at points of entry
and accompany with G and D$_7$ chord changing at half bar.
Another person could improvise on and about the note D.)
Kookaburra
(Chord pattern ‖: D G | D D :‖. Sing and accompany with
outline melodies drawn from each line and played on
different instruments.)
London's Burning
(G and D$_7$ chords lasting 2 and 1 beats respectively. The
'Fire fire' may be played on a bell-like instrument.)

11. Sing Care Away, Book *1*
(Novello)
Begone Dull Care
(2 chords G and D$_7$ mostly 2 chords per bar except in 3rd line.)
Past Three o'Clock
(First 2 bars will act as ostinato throughout. Fairly easy
melody to chorus D–D without F sharp.)
The Campbells are Comin'
(Rhythmic additions and ostinato.)
The Ash Grove
(3 chords G, D$_7$ and C. 1 chord per bar. Use D$_7$ in 7th, 15th
and penultimate bars. Omit chord from bar with C sharp
and play note A only, followed by D chord without 7th in
next bar.)
The Fiddler
(2 notes or chords G and D$_7$. Improvise passage round note D.)
Sur le Pont d'Avignon
(By rebarring so that it becomes:

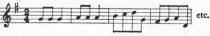

it is easy to use 2 chords G and D$_7$.)

97

12. Something to Sing
Brace (Cambridge)

(Includes many suggestions by the compiler in the full music edition and guitar chords in the vocal edition.)

The Gypsy Davey
(2 chords.)

Jesse James
(3 chords G, D_7 and C.)

Old Joe Clarke
(Effective with drone on D and A changing to C and G where marked with guitar chord C. Good for *ad lib.* rhythm work.)

Out in the Great Northwest
(Off-beat percussion, 3 chords D, A_7 and G.)

Old Paint
(Easy melody for instruments. Works well with instrumental descant mostly a third above, but where tune has low D use A not F sharp. 2 chords G and D_7.)

13. Songs for Juniors
Horton (Schofield & Sims)

The London Watchman's Song
(First 2 bars suitable for ostinato throughout. Easy melody to chorus D–D without F sharp.)

The Carrion Crow
(Last 2 bars as rhythmic ostinato.)

Gathering Apples
(Ostinato of doh–soh (E–B) in dotted minims.)

There's a Hole in my Bucket
(3 chords in C. Use G_7 in 3rd whole bar of tune and F–G_7 in 7th bar. Would at a pinch work with 2 chords only if G_7 was used for whole of 7th bar.)

Oh Dear what can the Matter be
(3 chords in F. I | I | V_7 | V_7 | I | I | IV V_7 | I.)

14. The Song Tree
Hitchcock (Curwen)

(N.B. in this book the guitar chords are added over the vocal
line. Beware when 'Capo' at such and such a fret is mentioned,
as in No. 3, as this will mean that these chords played on
other instruments would not fit the melody if played in the
key printed.)

Morning
(Easy rhythm, 3 chords only.)

Tulips in Holland
(Will work well with just G and D_7 chords, e.g. G – – |
G – – | D_7 – – | D_7 – – | etc.)

Mr Ragamuffin
(Regular chord or bass-note pattern, suitable for 2 chime
bars or timpani, on F F C F which repeats 4 times.)

Queen Mary
(3 chords—all marked.)

My Papa
(Catchy rhythm providing suitable figures for improvised
percussion accompaniment.)

Kolyada
(1 D chord fits whole song, or drone/ostinato built on D
and A.)

Skip to my Lou
(A great favourite. 2 chords G and D_7 also improvise round
note D.)

15. Fifty Songs for Schools
(Associated Board)

Early one Morning
(3 chords, 1 per bar except in 7th bar. Use IV in bar 14
treating E and C as accented passing notes.)

Begone Dull Care
(2 chords F and C_7, mostly 2 chords per bar.)

The Miller of Dee

(Ostinato fits throughout, but some may

prefer to omit from 'and this the burden, etc.'.)

Here's a Health unto His Majesty
   (Simple tune, 3 notes only in first two phrases. Later,
   substitution of C for top E would make it easier for recorders.)

The British Grenadiers
   (Good for rhythmic accompaniment, might add

| ⁊ ♫ ♪⁊ |

Bobby Shafto
   (2 chords in G.)

Hot Cross Buns
   (5 notes G–D plus lower D.)

(Also useful songs in French and German.)

Six useful Carols from various sources

Silent Night
   (3 chords in Key C. As tune is wide ranging sing it, but
   perhaps add easier 2nd part for instruments derived from the
   chord notes.)

I Saw Three Ships
   (2 chords I and V.)

Infant Holy, Infant Lowly
   (Pitch in Key G and work out accompaniment with lower
   D, G and A following the tune outline for first 2 bars.)

We Three Kings
   (Works with drones. Change for chorus. Easy tune.)

Masters in this Hall
   (Ostinato.)

Hydom, Hydom, Tydlidom
   (Good for rhythmic accompaniment and drone.)

(Avoid the Christmas Hymn type of carol as the harmonies change
too frequently and irregularly to be effective with chimes, etc.)

Six useful Nursery Rhymes from various sources

Little Jack Horner
   (2 chords in key F or G, in alternate bars, starting unusually
   with V_7.)

Lavender's Blue
   (Easy tune, 3 chords.)
Oranges and Lemons
   (Effective with drone, change to lower drone in middle.)
Little Bo-Peep
   (If in key F use accompaniment of 2 chimes playing F and C;
   try to keep a fairly regular pattern to make it easier to
   remember.)
Hickory Dickory Dock
   (Try a clock ticking ostinato on D and A.)
I Love Little Pussy
   (An easy 5-note tune in Key G, using 2 chords, again starting
   with V_7.)

Appendix B

Instrumental music suitable for arrangement for class use

A few pointers only are listed here. To be more definite in this
field is undesirable as the capabilities of different schools will vary
considerably and the choice from the works of the composer must
be left to the teacher.

The following composers have all written easy keyboard music
and reference to piano albums of their music selected for beginners
will reveal useful material.

Thomas Arne

J. S. Bach (and Family)

Bartok

Beethoven (dances)

J. C. Faber

Handel

James Hook

Mozart (early works)

Purcell (suites)

Schubert (dances)

Schumann (Album for the
Young)

Sonatina Composers,
e.g. Clementi, Kuhlau,
Diabelli duets.

D. G. Türk

Reference to the numerous albums of classics for young pianists
will also be worthwhile when hunting for music, as also will a
look at recorder albums, particularly those which include simple
ensemble arrangements. A few of the latter are listed below.

The First Ensemble Book: GIESBERT	(Schott)
From a Music Book of 1740	(Bärenreiter)
Pleasure and Practice with the Recorder,	
Book 2 : L. WINTERS	(Arnold)
Read and Play, Books 1 and 2 :	
L. and G. WINTERS	(Galliard)
School Ensemble Book: BERGMANN	(Schott)
Twelve Trios for Recorder Ensemble,	
Books 1 and 2 : BENOY	(Oxford)

Dance Manuals such as *Community Dance Manuals*, 1–6, and *Swing
Partners* published by The English Folk Dance and Song Society
are also useful.

Appendix C

How to start instrumental work with a limited budget
(Prices are necessarily approximate as there is a variation between the manufacturers.)

For £15

	£	p
10 Chime Bars C,D,E,F♯,G,A,B,C′, and D′ plus another G. Approximately £1 each	10	0
1 Descant Recorder		90
1 Tambourine (10 inch)	2	25
1 Triangle (4 inch)		25
1 Triangle (6 inch)		30
1 pair Indian Bells		60
1 pair Plastic Maracas		70
	15	0

For £37

	£	p
14 Chime Bars. C,D,E,F♯,G,A,B,C′, and D′, plus another G as before and in addition F♮, B♭, C♯ and E′. Approximately £1 each	14	0
3 Descant Recorders (15s each)	2	70
1 Large or Alto 13-note Glockenspiel	8	0
1 set of 3 extra bars B♭ and 2 F♯s for above	1	0
1 small 20-note chromatic Glockenspiel	4	0
1 Tambourine (10 inch)	2	25
1 Solo Triangle (6 inch)		90
1 Solo Triangle (8 inch)	1	10
1 pair Indian Bells		60
1 pair Maracas		70
1 Tambour (hand drum) (12 inch)	1	75
	37	0

If another £3 were available I would either put it towards improved quality in the percussion, or towards a fund to buy a pair of school timpani or a xylophone.

Appendix D

Brief bibliography (excluding music)

J. BLADES, *Orchestral Percussion Technique* (Oxford University Press)

K. BLOCKSIDGE, *How to Use Melodic Percussion Instruments* (Nursery School Association)

K. BLOCKSIDGE, *Making Musical Apparatus and Instruments* (Nursery School Association)

D. HALL, *Music for Children*, Teacher's Manual to *Orff-Schulwerk* (Schott)

A. LOMAX, *American Folk Guitar* (Robbins Music)

A. MENDOZA and J. RIMMER, *On the Beat* (Boosey & Hawkes) (A section of five-note tunes with accompaniments is available separately.)

R. ROBERTS, *Musical Instruments Made to be Played* (Dryad)

R. M. THACKRAY, *Creative Music in Education* (Novello)

Appendix E

1. Musical arrangements and compositions for class use

Ding Dong Bell, Books 1 and 2: Y. ADAIR	(Novello)
Graded Rounds, with optional tuned percussion: A. MENDOZA	(Novello)
Make Your Own Music: D. MACMAHON	(Leeds Music)
Music and Rhythm: P. REDER	(Novello)
Music for Children: C. ORFF	(Schott)
Vol. 1, *Pentatonic*;	
Vol. 2, *Drone Bass*;	
Vol. 3, *Dominant and Sub-dominant*	
On the Beat, words and melody: A. MENDOZA and J. RIMMER	(Boosey & Hawkes)
Rejoice and Be Merry (10 *carols*): arr. G. WINTERS	(Chappell)
Rhymes with Chimes: O REES and A. MENDOZA	(Oxford U.P.)
Shepherds in the Manger: F. DINN	(Schott)
The Shepherds' Tale or Caedmon: I. KENDELL (Junior Music Series)	(Chester)
Sing It and Ring It: G. WINTERS	(Universal)
Sing Play: E. STEPHENSON	(Hohner)
Sing with Chimes: Books 1 and 2: O. REES	(Oxford U.P.)
Songs to Sing and Play: A. BENTLEY	(Novello)
Songs and Tunes for Junior Ensemble: O. REES and A. MENDOZA	(Oxford U.P.)
A Suite of Numbers: G. WINTERS	(Galliard)
Thirty Folk Settings for Children: A. MENDOZA and J. RIMMER	(Curwen)

2. Musical arrangements and compositions for more advanced class use or follow-up work

Ahmet the Woodseller: G. CROSSE	(Oxford U.P.)
Bobby Shafto: E. WEBB	(Schott)
Carol Suite: P. PFAFF	(Boosey & Hawkes)
Festive March: G. WINTERS	(Galliard)
Five Folk Songs: B. BONSOR	(Oxford U.P.)
Five French Dances of 1750 (inc. parts):	
A. MENDOZA	(Schott)
A Folk Song Suite: P. PFAFF	(Boosey & Hawkes)
The Little School Orchestra (Series):	
J. MAINWARING	(Paxton)
The Midnight Thief: R. R. BENNETT	(Mills)
Nursery Frolic: J. BELL	(Chappell)
Playing for Pleasure: F. DINN	(Schott)
Books 1 and 2,	
Psalm 150: B. BRITTEN	(Boosey & Hawkes)
Rondeau from Abdelazar by Purcell:	
arr. B. BONSOR	(Oxford U.P.)
Soldiers March by Schumann: arr. with	
variation, G. WINTERS	(Galliard)
Some Birds and Beasts: I. A. COPLEY	(Chappell)
A Spring Cantata: I. KENDELL	(Chester)
Square Dance Tunes: — SALKELD	(Mills)
Three Folk Tunes: F. DINN	(Schott)
Three Pieces by Jeremiah Clarke:	
G. WINTERS	(Oxford U.P.)
Variations on a French Tune: G. WINTERS	(Galliard)
Waltz in D major by Mozart:	
arr. K. BLOCKSIDGE	(Cramer)
The Year. G. WINTERS	(Oxford U.P.)

  * Includes a part for voices